Software Portability
and Standards

ELLIS HORWOOD SERIES IN COMPUTERS AND THEIR APPLICATIONS

Series Editor: Brian Meek, Director of the Computer Unit, Queen Elizabeth College, University of London

ELLIS HORWOOD BOOKS IN COMPUTING

Software
Portability
and Standards

INGEMAR DAHLSTRAND, M.Sc.
Systems Analyst
Lund University Computing Centre
Sweden

ELLIS HORWOOD LIMITED
Publishers · Chichester

Halsted Press: a division of
JOHN WILEY & SONS
New York · Chichester · Brisbane · Toronto

First published in 1984 by
ELLIS HORWOOD LIMITED
Market Cross House, Cooper Street, Chichester, West Sussex, PO19 1EB, England

The publisher's colophon is reproduced from James Gillison's drawing of the ancient Market Cross, Chichester.

Distributors:

Australia, New Zealand, South-east Asia:
Jacaranda-Wiley Ltd., Jacaranda Press,
JOHN WILEY & SONS INC.,
G.P.O. Box 859, Brisbane, Queensland 40001, Australia

Canada:
JOHN WILEY & SONS CANADA LIMITED
22 Worcester Road, Rexdale, Ontario, Canada.

Europe, Africa:
JOHN WILEY & SONS LIMITED
Baffins Lane, Chichester, West Sussex, England.

North and South America and the rest of the world:
Halsted Press: a division of
JOHN WILEY & SONS
605 Third Avenue, New York, N.Y. 10016, U.S.A.

© 1984 I. Dahlstrand/

British Library Cataloguing in Publication Data
Dahlstrand,
Software po
(Ellis Horwood
1. Software compatability
I. Title
001.64'25   QA76.6

ISBN 0-85312-642-9 (Ellis Horwood Limited)
ISBN 0-470-20083-9 (Halsted Press)

Typeset by Ellis Horwood Limited.
Printed in Great Britain by R.J. Acford, Chichester.

Contents

Introduction

My interest in portability and standards is of long standing. When my working life started in 1955 at the Saab Aircraft Company, the first electronic computer in Sweden, BESK, had been in operation for two years. Copies of BESK were being built at Saab, at the University of Lund, at Regnecentralen in Copenhagen, and at Facit Electronics in Stockholm. The cooperation between these groups made for a lively, intellectually stimulating environment. Our superintendent, Mr. Börje Langefors, at this early time inspired us to think beyond the manual machine coding that was the only tool available in those days and to plan for 'automatic coding', as it was then called.

At some point of time during this project, the people from Regnecentralen proposed to introduce index registers in the new computers and to re-number the machine operations to make them more systematic and thus easier to remember. A lively debate broke out between those who thought this was a good idea and those who argued for building an exact copy of BESK in order to preserve compatibility and free exchange of programs. Like many other debates on intellectual topics, this one grew very heated. Resignations were offered; tempers flared. Thus we came to grips very early with the issue of *progress versus standards*. In the end, all of the BESK copiers went their own ways except for the people at Facit. By sticking to strict compatibility with the BESK already in operation they maintained a computing environment in Stockholm that coordinated almost all scientific and technical programming in Sweden for close to ten years and resulted in a very large, useful program library.

In 1962 the BESK-Facit epoch was brought to an end by a new breed of computers: the IBM 7090, the Univac 1107, the CDC 3600, the GE 625. We were faced with the huge task of converting our program library for these computers. Though we had implemented Algol in 1961 (that was my task within the company), most of the library was still in machine code. A concerted conversion to some common Fortran or Algol dialect would have been appropriate. Through lack of resources and foresight, no such effort was made. Not only did many of the programs expire; the cooperation around the library that had come naturally because of strict compatibility broke up, never to be restored. As if the existence of different Fortran dialects were not enough, the job control languages that came with the new machines completed the splitting of our computing community into hermetically isolated groups. The waste was appalling. This was when I decided to get to work as soon as possible on the problems of compatibility and standards.

My next ten years, however, had to be centred on a fairly conventional administrative career. I supervised a group of applications programmers at Facit, and from 1968 led the build-up of a university computing centre in Lund. Not until 1974 could I start the work on 'Portability in Technical and Scientific ADP' on a grant from STU, the Swedish Board for Technical Development. In this study I found I had to attack three problem areas at the same time: programming language, control language and representation of data. Standards had to be investigated for quality and acceptance; alternatives had to be proposed where standards were not enough. This work continued, on and off, until 1980, when the theoretical problems posed in the study seemed to me to be essentially solved. I decided to resign as director of the Computing Centre and return to applications programming to test the ideas collected during the study. The present book is the result of the study and the following field work.

The study passed through four distinct stages. All of these, perhaps excepting the first one, are to some degree reflected in this book. To start with, I investigated the use of machine independent intermediate languages as a tool for constructing portable Algol and Fortran compilers. Realising the outstanding importance of Fortran, I concentrated next on implementing machine independent Fortran and command languages through pre-compilers; simultaneously I experimented with porting data. As international work went forward and looked more and more promising, my attention focussed on standards work; finally, during the field work in programming, I have become painfully aware of the continuing need for languages that are not only portable but also safe and convenient to use.

This book tries to stick to the problems of daily computing as perceived by the application programmer. At the computing centre where I work, application programming is organised as an independent economic unit which means we have to be practical if we want to earn our keep. Much of what goes on in the language world happens far above our heads; from our point of view a language exists if, and only if, our current manufacturer supplies it. Over the years I have come into contact with many of the fields of application computing. These include numerical computation, statistics, information retrieval, graphics, linguistics, and even some billing and sales statistics. On the other hand, I have little or no experience of real-time, networking, protection issues and data base management. Apart from an occasional Cobol or APL program, my programs have been written in various vintages of Algol and Fortran. Fortran has a dominating place in the text, both because it is the one tool you are always sure to have – and be allowed to use! – and because it is actually in many respects a very good tool.

This book assumes that you, the reader, have some working knowledge of computers. You may have just run a few Fortran programs or you may have worked in the field for a long time. You are not quite satisfied with the state of computing, or you would not have bothered to open this book. Most of the book is in a conversational tone. It does not propose exact solutions, rather it tries to identify the issues – technical, commercial and human – that influence portability and standards. It tries to point out what you can do about it at your own installation; what you can expect standards bodies and manufacturers to do; what you will have to push them to do.

As you will see from the sequel, there remains a lot of pushing.

Acknowledgements

The computer community is a very open one. Ideas are born, elaborated and exchanged in a continuous flow. No project could be carried on without depending heavily on this international background. A complete list of inspirators to this book would be very long indeed. I will therefore restrict myself to acknowledging the help I have received through personal contacts.

I wish to thank

Professors Börje Langefors and Carl Eric Fröberg for introducing me to computing in an intellectually stimulating atmosphere;

the late Dr. Olle Karlqvist for making me conscious of standards;

the Swedish Board for Technical Development (STU) for generously funding my research;

Mr. Arne Sundström for taking on a double work load during my leaves of absence;

Messrs. Brian Meek, David Hill and Magnus Tideman for reading the manuscript and discussing the ideas in it;

Messrs. Jan Nordling and Jean Persson for continuing moral support.

1

Some first principles

And the LORD said:
"Behold, they all have one language and one speech and from now on
nothing shall be impossible for them".

From Genesis, Tower of Babel

1.1 WHAT IS PORTABILITY?

Any study of a large and complex subject will have to start out by delimiting
the scope of work and making some definitions.

What is portability? Broadly speaking, it is the ability to move an application from one computer to another unchanged and get the same results. We used
to call this 'compatibility' and it is not altogether clear why the new term
'portability' was introduced. Perhaps it was intended to point out that portability
could be in the software instead of in the hardware. Portability could be measured
as the percentage of lines that could be left unchanged when porting an application, and so it became a relative property rather than an absolute one. Perhaps
people were just tired of the old term and needed a new buzz word.

To talk only of moving programs would be too restrictive. Data and
command language sequences must be portable too; in fact, as soon as command
languages appeared they became a greater obstacle to portability than the other
two. Tackling all three problem areas at one time sounds rather ambitious but is
necessary to attain full portability. In addition, there are several problem areas
that have not been taken up in a systematic manner in standards bodies because
they fall in the border zone between two of the areas or all three. An example of
this is the control of margins in printing: is this a command language or programming language function? Or the control of the collating sequence, i.e. the
order of sorting, which area does that belong to?

More for reasons of my background than anything else, the study centered
on technical and scientific ADP. This is an area where a lot of people write their
own programs without being computer professionals. The different areas of computing do, however, have the same problems to a high degree; the conclusions
reached hold for administrative ADP as well.

In another sense the level of ambition of the study had to stay low. There
was no prospect that the study would have much impact on manufacturers and
standards bodies, so whatever was accomplished had to be practical while it was
being used and reasonably easy to convert once the problems had been solved
internationally.

17

To get back to the definition, it says 'give the same results'. This has to be interpreted within the bounds of reason. One would hardly say portability had been damaged if system printouts were not quite the same throughout, as long as they were reasonably similar. Neither could we expect to get exactly the same digits in a result computed by real arithmetic on two different machines.

Real arithmetic is the art of getting useful results from operations that have some degree of imprecision. In fact, I sometimes think it would not hurt to have the computer truncate our results on Monday, Wednesday and Friday and round them on the other days. It would be slightly baffling to start with, but would serve as a constant reminder of the gap between computer printouts and reality.

So our complete definition reads: 'Portability is the degree to which you can move an application to another computer and get essentially the same results'.

Under what conditions can this be done? One condition, which is so self-evident that we rarely mention it, is that the programs should be in *source form*. That is behind the whole concept of high-level languages and any form of portability. Similarly, data files have to be in *text form* (character form, formatted, however you wish to call them). There is no way binary files could be moved automatically between different machines. But this condition is not sufficient. If you have, say, a payroll in full operation, a certain run on the computer may consist of executing a ready-made program merging two files and producing a third one. This run alone is not portable, because a run depends on a whole system of files being present and on the existence of compiled programs and libraries. The porting will have to be a porting of the whole application: source programs, libraries, data and all; and the whole application has to be loaded and started up. This has nothing to do with differences between machines. You would have to do the very same thing if your computer broke down and you had to move to a similar reserve machine. This discussion leads us to the concept of a *normal form*, which will be discussed more in the command language chapter.

Another important concept that turned up early was the distinction between *algorithmic*, *optimising*, and *environmental* information.

It was probably an APL course that started me on this track. APL is a very neat, compact language. All sorts of applications can be described in APL and seemingly in a machine independent fashion. I started to wonder what made this particular language different. Why could APL get away with storing an array where there had been a string a moment before, and get exactly the right size to it, neither more nor less? Why could it compile and execute a program or procedure in the same simple call when other languages had to leave this task to complex, wildly different command language sequences? Part of the answer was of course that APL was allowed to be less efficient. It did not reserve space for an array at compile time, so more administration had to be done at run time. It could not perform compilation as a separate operation, so it had to interpret the program every time it was run. APL did not care about optimising. All commands were there solely to influence the result. By contrast, other programming languages and control languages contained a mixture of algorithmic information and information with other purposes, mainly optimisation and environment control.

This distinction is going to play an important part throughout this book, so a complete explanation with examples is called for. Let us first consider the statement 'X = X + 2.5'. This is an obvious example of an algorithmic statement. It computes something and changes the value of a variable.

Next, consider the declaration 'REAL A(12)'. What does it achieve? If you have never thought about it before, you would probably answer something like: 'It reserves twelve cells for the array A and implies that all future operations on A be in floating-point'. I agree. The question is, is this part of the algorithm? I would argue against that. A reasonably clever system would find out when A was being created, how many cells it needed, and make space for it. But this might mean some reorganising of memory, so the system must retain the ability to reorganise memory throughout the execution of the program. Therefore the system can be made more efficient by forcing the programmer to give so much information beforehand that the memory can be organised once and for all at compile time. Hence the declaration 'REAL A(12)' is essentially an attempt to optimise (and a rather poor one at that, as we shall see later on).

Again, consider the declaration 'INTEGER I'. It reserves one cell for I and implies that all future operations on I be in integer arithmetic. Since most machines have faster integer arithmetic than real arithmetic, this would seem a valid optimisation, and makes it possible to choose the arithmetic for each operation at compile time. The declaration is not, however, completely without an algorithmic effect, since the statement 'I = X + 2.5' will now include an implicit truncation or rounding of the result before storing it in I. So this declaration 'INTEGER I' contains both optimising and algorithmic information. (It is only fair to note that occasionally integer arithmetic is used in order to obtain exact arithmetic, in which case the algorithmic effect is the main goal.)

As an example of environmental information, take the response you give when your system asks you for user identification and the password. This information obviously neither contributes to the result, nor makes it come about more efficiently. It just ensures that you are authorised to use the system and tells it who is going to pay.

I am very much tempted to include another category of information, exemplified by the PREP directive on the system I use at present. (I am sure you can find a parallel on yours!) Like most systems, ours has an intermediate stage between compilation and execution, called mapping (or linkage). At this stage you can give the system a program file from which to select subprograms that will be needed during execution but have not been included in the source code. In order to be used as a library, the program file must have an 'Entry Point Table' which you create with the PREP directive. If the file is not PREPped, the mapping is aborted, i.e. terminated with an error report.

This is preposterous. Since there is no alternative to PREPping in this case, and no other situation in which you want to PREP, it is obvious that the mapping processor should do it for you. So the PREP directive – along with dozens of similar ones – belongs to the category *unnecessary* information; it tells the system something it ought to find out for itself.

Once this distinction has been drawn, we can start thinking about portability in a much more orderly manner.

The algorithmic information can be made 100% portable. If we want to describe an application that reads text files, processes them and outputs resulting text files, there is no earthly reason why it can't be done machine independently.

The optimising information is inherently less portable. To begin with, what we want to optimise may vary considerably from one machine to another. If you have a small, fast machine your optimum will be different from what it is if you have a large, slow machine. If you have programmed floating-point, you have much more reason to use integer arithmetic, whenever possible, than if you have built-in floating-point. And so on. But we can retain a lot of portability even for this kind of information if we are careful about the manner in which we give it: it should be given in as standard and machine independent form as possible.

The environmental information is essentially non-portable. It embodies the information that we must, or may even want to, change when we move an application to another machine. So again our level of ambition is that the *form* of the information should be as standard as possible.

20

Now let me make another point about portability: *Programs cannot be ported unchanged, unless they are prepared for it.* If you have worked with conversion you will know. But it is in no way self-evident. In the course of my project work, I was often asked: 'So you will be able to convert our programs to machine so-and-so?'. Unfortunately that is not possible. A command language sequence, or even a program in a Fortran dialect, is not just another way of instructing 'the same' underlying system. The underlying system is always slightly different from machine to machine. To get a safe conversion you would have to simulate the underlying system, warts and all, which is clumsy and expensive. Alternatively, you can make a raw conversion and flag suspicious places in the code. These will have to be treated by an intelligent person who will most likely have to know something about the application. If you want easy portability, you will have to start with defining a machine independent system, an abstract machine, you want to instruct. Then you can write portable programs for it, and translate them automatically. But the old programs will just have to be taken care of the hard way.

1.2 THE IMPACT OF PORTABILITY

Easy portability would have a strong impact on computing. We are so used to the present state of affairs that it takes a conscious effort of imagination to wrench loose and see things as they might be. So, just to get worked up for the sequel, let us take a flight of fancy.

The most immediate boon would be that we could move jobs from machine to machine. This covers a whole gamut of situations. Our usual machine could be overloaded, while another is almost empty. Or it could have a breakdown. Our program might call for an unusual amount of storage or some exotic plotting device. Whatever the reason we would be freed from the fences between one installation and the next that are so much a part of today's landscape that we hardly see them.

Buying a new computer would be a very much easier task than today. It would be easier to compare the machines offered, and, having chosen one, to install and load it.

Education of people in computer use would be easier and more to the point. The portability of programs would be mirrored by a portability of people.

The market for software products would be changed drastically. A good program would have a market much broader and more long-lasting than now. We have seen approaches to such large-scale markets in mini-computers. Portability would make it happen across the board.

When I started the portability project, I was asked to calculate how much time was actually being spent on program (and people) conversion in Sweden. I could estimate that for technical and scientific ADP alone, the cost was in the order of $1 million a year. But we have already seen from the above that actual conversion costs do not begin to measure the impact of portability. It is like trying to measure the value of a standard railway gauge by measuring actual re-loading costs in the year 1850! We do not know what they were, and having seen the railways transform society, we do not care.

1.3 PREPARING FOR PORTABILITY

What practical steps can we then take to prepare for program porting? Some ideas will be presented here in the form of advice to a programmer team or its management.

The first general piece of advice is: find out what the standard is. Surprisingly few people know — unless one has personal experience of a conversion, one is apt to take one's current supplier's manual as the norm. (The numbers of some relevant standards will be given in the respective chapters.)

Secondly, it is well to supplement the standard with some manual which points out how to apply the standard to achieve portable programs. Because of implementation differences and deficiencies in the standards, mere adherence to standard does not guarantee portability. Being aware of the standard and its limitations is, however, a long step forward. You can, at an early stage, visualise the changes you will have to make when porting the system and try to:

(1) minimise the types of changes necessary;
(2) concentrate the ones you cannot avoid into as few places as possible and comment them.

If portability is a daily concern for you, you may even consider writing some pre-compilers to aid conversion. With the steady advance of compiling techniques, this is no longer the major undertaking it used to be, and it is very useful to give substance to your ideas. A converter of course does not have to be

100% automatic. It should always contain some feature to request additional information from the user about constructs that are difficult to translate and to allow the user to put some finishing touches to the product.

When you are lucky enough to know from the beginning two or more installations where the programs are to be used, you can develop and test them in parallel on these systems. In this way you will be made conscious of problems at an early stage, which may save extensive rewriting and even redesigning of the system later on.

1.4 STANDARDS WORK

Next, I would like to say a few words about standards work.

1.4.1 Purpose of Standards

Standards have several purposes besides the obvious and economically very important one of portability.

· For instance, in industrial real time control, portability of programs is a secondary consideration; the important thing is what we might call portability of people, a common language and a shared set of concepts to start working from.

A third important purpose is the setting of quality standards (where we have not yet got very far), minimum levels of, for example, generality, consistency, naturalness in languages. We would not be happy with a standard that did allow porting of programs but made them unreasonably hard to write.

A standard may assure us of a minimum level of performance and safety, for example, require that unexpected run-time errors should be reported to the user. There has been a long discussion on whether error action should be included in standards. On the one hand attempts to specify error messages in Fortran have broken down, because every error turned out to be somebody's extension. On the other hand, in command language committees there is no doubt error messages or, more generally, response language, has to be included in the standard; the same attitude is taken by the Basic and Pascal standards. There is a consensus by now, however, that:

— errors should be reported unless obscured by other errors;
— a high level of readability is required of error reports;

— an undefined language construct should either be reported as an error or explicitly be an allowable extension; and last but not least,
— error handling is indeed within the scope of standards.

An oft-debated question is: do standards impede progress?

If you standardise too early, the technical content of the standard may be weak; if you wait too long it may be hard to change established local practices. Some people feel that standards do indeed inhibit new features and experimentation; others point out that committees further the exchange of new ideas, and even add features to their languages that have never been implemented before. A good case can be made for permissive languages; almost any language can develop a lot through pre-compilers and macro facilities without unduly impairing the primary purpose of standardisation.

1.4.2 How the Work is Done

Standards committees work in different ways according to the current situation.

Rarely does a committee think up a new language on its own. Its first priority is, and should undoubtedly be, to follow the spontaneous development of a language that occurs through implementation and extension and standardise on the basis of that. Second, it may go beyond current practice and improve the language on its own. One sometimes wonders where the process of improving a language ends. That, of course, depends on what you mean by 'improvement'.

If you remove a restriction from a language, perhaps because you have gained a better understanding of compiling techniques, or because the efficiency gained through the restriction is marginal; then you undoubtedly improve the language, and in a way that converges quite rapidly. An example is the way Fortran 77 permits the use of integer-valued expressions in places where Fortran 66 allowed only constants or only variables or only linear functions of those.

On the other hand, the continuous addition of new features to a language must be kept on a tight rein. As often as not, these are stop-gap measures made necessary by some poor design decision at an early stage in the development of the language. They do not cure the basic flaws of the language. This kind of improvement is never-ending. A case in point is the FORMAT facility of Fortran which seems to live a life of its own, steadily accumulating new frills.

Considering the limited resources that go into standards work, we really cannot afford piecemeal improvement. More work should be put into the development of a few, but well thought out, basic language features. I think this will be a slow, but rewarding, process, which will give us a foundation to build application software on. There is really no alternative to concentrating the resources like this. If we spread them too thin to do the work well, it will have to be done again.

For the same reason, limited resources, we really ought to standardise as few languages as possible, and apply them as widely as possible. This might seem heavy-handed, but in the end we shall probably have to do just this. Perhaps too much work had gone into standardisation of languages, as opposed to other software, like word processing, sort/merge, file updating and archiving, etc.

The standardisation of computer languages takes place in an environment that is dominated by one manufacturer to an unusual degree. An interesting question is: Has this helped or hindered standardisation? On the one hand, IBM languages, dialects or codes have a strong tendency to become *de facto* standards; on the other hand, when there really is a need to give and take to achieve standard, it is very difficult actually to change the practices of IBM and its customers.

Most computer standards have been American standards. The normal lifetime for such a standard is 5 years, after which time it should be confirmed, replaced or withdrawn. This time scale is surely too short for language standards. If a standard is submitted to a major rewrite (e.g. Fortran 77) you need to let the circulation of a draft produce a number of proposals that are then sent out for a straw vote. After the new standard is adopted you will need the feed-back that results when a major part of the user community has been exposed to implementations of the new standard, including a feeling of whether the old standard is being superseded. This means 10, rather than 5 years between major rewrites. Other things, like writing common extensions into the standard, might be done on a considerably shorter time-scale, perhaps in the form of additions/appendices to the standard.

One thing we do not know how to do yet is to phase out obsolete language features. We usually try to put them in special section of the standard. This does not always help if the feature has a widespread use.

1.4.3 The Form and Contents of a Standard

A precise description of a standard is very important. This can be achieved through a good metalanguage, at least as far as syntax is concerned. So far, we have had a different metalanguage for each programming language, but research is going on to create a common metalanguage; one candidate is British Standard BS 6154. A metalanguage is an exact and compact language description directed primarily to the implementor. A user who has not used metalanguage before will need a less formal description. If the language description is understandable enough, you can throw away the manual when you have mastered it, and use the language description to look up moot points. Defining the syntax is, comparatively speaking, the easy part; the hard part is to define the semantics strictly. I have used examples rather than metalanguage in this book, but then its primary purpose is not to define languages.

In the early days, a standard usually contained a hardware representation, but this seems to be one problem that is slowly losing importance, because everybody is getting to use more or less the same, reasonably rich, character set.

Language standards (the kind that give true portability) are only the first step towards performance standards. If you have portability, you can start to design test batches and compare the time and cost of running them on different systems; and then you may start to find out how many different kinds, or aspects, of performance a hardware/software system may have. We might one day be able to measure a system's performance at number crunching, string handling, I/O, etc., separately from each other; this would be a great aid to the computer buyer.

1.4.4 Validation and Enforcement

A standard cannot be enforced if it cannot be validated. We need facilities in compilers to validate programs; and we need validation suites to validate compilers, perhaps also institutions responsible for doing so. This also sets higher requirements for the form of the standard. Enforcement by lawsuit is getting to be possible in principle, but the main enforcement will still some through ordinary user pressure; and it should be applied! Official validation of compilers has been going on for years, often by military institutions which are large computer buyers. Examples of this are Cobol, Fortran, Coral 66, Pascal and recently Ada.

1.4.5 Relations between Standards

Standards inevitably have a relation to one another. It is important that different languages can use the same files. It is also very convenient if programs in one language can call subprograms in another language.

The ideal solution seems to be a standard interface, i.e. a procedure call and parameter passing mechanism. Things like internal representation of data will also have to be the same in different languages on the same system. Other central standards, besides procedure interfaces, are character set and command language standards.

A recent problem is that new features like graphics and data base handling are added as new statements to languages. This is convenient for the user but may result in enormous overlaps. Ways of avoiding this are discussed in later chapters.

Much of what was said here is based on a discussion of standards within the framework of [1]. If you have a particular interest in these matters, a detailed discussion between experts is to be found in that book. A short guide to standards with particular emphasis on their practical application and their strictness is [2].

1.5 REFERENCES

[1] I. D. Hill & B. L. Meek (eds.), *Programming Language Standardisation*, Ellis Horwood Ltd (publ.), Chichester, 1980.
[2] B. L. Meek, *Guides to Computing Standards*, No. 15, *Programming Languages*, National Computing Centre, Sep. 1981.

A number of ANS and ISO standards and draft proposals will be mentioned in the text. These are available, respectively, from:

— American National Standards Institute, 1430 Broadway, New York.
— International Organisation for Standardisation, Geneva.

2

Data representation

This chapter is going to be short. Nowadays data representation is fairly well standardised and not nearly the obstacle to portability it used to be.

The topic can be divided into three: internal representation, punched cards, and tape labelling.

2.1 INTERNAL REPRESENTATION

By internal representation we understand the manner in which characters, as we humans know them, are represented internally in a computer by a binary code. The first code schemes that were established were 6-bit representations. This allowed representation of 64 characters and thus could cover one case of the roman alphabet, the ten decimal digits, the blank, and a collection of miscellaneous characters like plus, minus, asterisk, etc. The Fieldata and BCD code were examples of such coding schemes.

With the advent of printers that could print both cases of letters, these schemes became too narrow. In 1966, ANSI adopted the ASCII code as an American national standard, which was also adopted as international standard as ISO 646 in 1969 [1]. This is a 7-bit scheme covering both cases of the alphabet and also a set of 32 control characters like carriage return, tabulation, bell, record separator, etc. Associated with ISO 646 is the standard ISO 2022 which defines ways of creating modified or extended character sets, and ISO 2375 which defines the procedure for registering such a new character set with ISO. Some 75 such new character sets, ranging from national alphabets over meteorological symbols to APL characters have been registered.

The ASCII standard code, though very good in itself, came just too late to win general acceptance. In the early sixties IBM had introduced the 8-bit EBCDIC code which spread rapidly and came close to becoming a *de facto* standard. This large user group, having just converted from BCD, had little incentive to switch to another code as long as IBM did not actively push it. The acceptance of the ASCII code therefore became a very slow process. By and by it gained acceptance among other manufacturers, among transmission people, and among minicomputers. Today, its eventual acceptance seems assured, but there is still a long way to go.

Happily, the ASCII code and the EBCDIC code comprise roughly the same character sets. A one-to-one translation is usually possible. So if the whole issue boiled down to a translation process, the problem would be rather small. But there are other issues to consider.

One issue is sorting. The internal representation defines an order between the characters, since each bit code corresponds to a certain numeric value. For instance, in the ASCII code blank is number 32, the digits are ranged from 48 to 57, the capital letters from 65 upward, etc. This 'collating sequence' becomes the natural way for the computer to compare characters when it sorts character strings. So if you move a data file to another computer, not only will you have to translate each character. You may have to re-sort the file too.

A second problem for people outside the English language area of the world is the placing of national letters, i.e. letters that appear in a country's alphabet but not in the English alphabet. Since this problem is connected with punched card codes, we shall briefly mention that aspect of data representation.

2.2 PUNCHED CARDS

The punched card codes went through an evolution similar to that of internal codes. The first punched card machines had very poor character sets. It could be just the digits and plus and minus. The minus sign was often punched over the last digit of a number. Then came the letters, implemented as double punches. Since some letters could be confused with a digit overpunched with a minus sign, you had to know which fields were alphabetic and which numeric. Up to now most card punches had the same codes. By and by other characters appeared, as double and triple punches. The 'other characters', however, were introduced in parallel by different manufacturers and turned out differently. By 1966, standardisation had progressed so far that a standard for punched card codes could be adopted and actually function as a standard [2]. This scheme contained the same characters as the internal ASCII code and was coordinated with it in other ways.

The ASCII code recognised the need for national letters and reserved three places for them in either case of the alphabet, where they were allowed to displace [, \,] and {, |, }, respectively. At a pinch you could also use @, `, and ^, ¯. These displaced characters were chosen with care to be the least necessary ones and were usually avoided (or at least substitutable) in programming languages.

But the national letters remained a problem. They had been introduced before the ASCII code in various countries and in various places in the coding scheme. In Sweden, for instance, the three letters Å, Ä and Ö were introduced in place of $, # and !. The same reasons that delayed the acceptance of the

ASCII code have made them remain there to this very day at EBCDIC installations. So at a Swedish EBCDIC installation $, # and ! will usually come out as letters, unless you switch to another printer chain with the English-American character set. This is obviously an obstacle to portability, in addition to being a bit of daily nuisance to the people concerned. No longer can you make a one-to-one translation between ASCII and EBCDIC. In order to port a data file you now need some idea whether $, #, ! appear in it in their international or national sense. In nasty cases they may quite possibly do both!

An appendix at the end of this chapter shows the standard character code and punched card code.

2.3 TAPE LABELLING

The third aspect to consider in data representation is tape labelling. Other properties of magnetic tape are very well standardised. Though the physical medium of tape has gone through a steady technical progress with densities increasing from 556 to 800 to 1600 to 6250 bits per inch, at every stage tapes as such have been physically portable. The problem has been the coding and organisation of the data on the tape.

At an early stage, installations started to use *tape labels*. A label is a block of 80 characters written before a file. Usually there are one or two volume labels heading the whole tape and telling us the tape's reel number, who is the owner of the tape, etc. Then each file on the tape has one or two file labels telling us the file's name, its blocking, etc. A standard for tape labelling was adopted, first by ANSI, then in 1969 by ISO as a recomendation ISO/R 1001 [3]. It was closely modelled on the IBM tape labelling system, and is generally adhered to by manufacturers. Its contribution to portability has, however, been most disappointing.

On the face of it, tape labelling ought to promote portability, and the introduction to ISO/R 1001 explicitly says so. On the face of it, it is a good idea to provide every tape with labels that identify it in case it is left lying about, and other labels that tell us how to interpret the information on the tape. What went wrong in practice?

The first mistake was that the standard was too permissive. Though recommending the ASCII code, it allowed the use of any other code. That made the tapes as unreadable at another installation as if there had been no standard.

The next problem was that it tried to be too many things at once. If we were to use the labels to further exchange of tapes, we should have needed ways to read and write labels under *program control,* so we could control the contents of the label and use those contents to influence the course of the program. But this is not how tape labels were implemented. Because tape labels from the start had an even more important function: they were to prevent people from using one another's tapes, intentionally or unintentionally. That meant the operating system should check that you had given the right labels and passwords and abort your run otherwise. To achieve this, the reading and writing of labels had to be under *operating system control.* And now the permissiveness of the standard wrought havoc. The standard was implemented differently in each place. Labels written at one site could not be read at another site. A revised, stricter version of the standard in 1976 [4] has not basically changed this fact.

I remember very well an attempt at tape interchange I undertook in 1975. I had managed to write an ASCII tape with labels on our Univac 1100 system – no mean achievement in itself since our system did not voluntarily write blocks of exactly 80 characters. I went up to our sister centre in Gothenburg which had an IBM 360/65 in order to have it read. Since it was an ASCII tape, I assigned it with the AL option.

Back came the run aborted with an error printout that sounded like a message from outer space. A friendly program librarian looked it up for me. It said I had used ANSI labels, and this installation was not configured for ANSI labels.

We next tried the NL (No Label) option. But the system was not to be fooled. It gave essentially the same reply: 'This is an ANSI tape – and I don't like ANSI tapes!'.

On the third try we used the BLP (Bypass Label Processing) option. This time the system swallowed hard and read. We had achieved a standard tape exchange, but at the price of overriding the normal security procedure of the centre.

A couple of years later a terse notice in the centre's newsletter informed the users that the BLP option was no longer available to them. From that day on, I have had a clear and easy recommendation for tape portability:

Use unlabelled EBCDIC tapes!

It is not smart. It is not good standards. It does not advance the world a step. But it has one compelling advantage. It works.

2.4 REFERENCES

[1] ISO 646—1973; 7-bit Coded Character Set for Information Processing Interchange.

[2] ISO 1679—1973; Information Processing — Representation of 7-bit Coded Character Set on 12-row Punched Cards.

[3] ISO/R 1001—1969; Magnetic Tape Labelling and File Structure for Information Interchange.

[4] ISO/DIS 1001.2—1976; Information Processing — Magnetic tape Labelling and File Structure for Information Interchange (Revision of [3]).

APPENDIX

TABLE OF ISO 646 CHARACTER CODE AND ISO 1679 PUNCHED CARD CODE

The table (opposite) illustrates the association between a numerical code, its meaning and the associated punched card code.

The numerical code corresponding to a box is its column index by 16, plus its row index. Each box contains, in its upper half the meaning of the numerical code associated with it, and in its lower half the punched card code associated with it.

To illustrate the placing of national letters and currency symbols, some boxes contain double meanings.

The abbreviations used for control characters (NUL, DLE, etc.) are explained below.

EXPLANATION OF ABBREVIATIONS

ACK	Acknowledge	GS	Group Separator
BEL	Bell	HT	Horizontal Tabulation
BS	Backspace	IS	Information Separator
CAN	Cancel	LF	Line Feed
CR	Carriage Return	NAK	Negative Acknowledge
DC	Device Control	NUL	Null
DEL	Delete	RS	Record Separator
DLE	Data Link Escape	SI	Shift In
EM	End of Medium	SO	Shift Out
ENQ	Enquiry	SOH	Start of Heading
EOT	End of Transmission	SP	Space
ESC	Escape	STX	Start of Text
ETB	End of Transmission Block	SUB	Substitute
ETX	End of Text	SYN	Synchronous Idle
FE	Format Effector	TC	Transmission Control
FF	Form Feed	US	Unit Separator
FS	File Separator	VT	Vertical Tabulation

36

	0	1	2	3	4	5	6	7
0	NUL 12-0-9-8-1	TC₇(DLE) 12-11-9-8-1	SP blank	0 0	@ É 8-4	P 11-7	` é 8-1	p 12-11-7
1	TC₁(SOH) 12-9-1	DC₁ 11-9-1	! 12-8-7	1 1	A 12-1	Q 11 8	a 12-0-1	q 12-11-8
2	TC₂(STX) 12-9-2	DC₂ 11-9-2	" 8-7	2 2	B 12-2	R 11-9	b 12-0-2	r 12-11-9
3	TC₃(ETX) 12-9-3	DC₃ 11-9-3	# 8-3	3 3	C 12-3	S 0-2	c 12-0-3	s 11-0-2
4	TC₄(EOT) 9-7	DC₄ 9-8-4	¤ $ 11-8-3	4 4	D 12-4	T 0-3	d 12-0-4	t 11-0-3
5	TC₅(ENQ) 0-9-8-5	TC₈(NAK) 9-8-5	% 0-8-4	5 5	E 12-5	U 0-4	e 12-0-5	u 11-0-4
6	TC₆(ACK) 0-9-8-6	TC₉(SYN) 9-2	& 12	6 6	F 12-6	V 0-5	f 12-0-6	v 11-0-5
7	BEL 0-9-8-7	TC₁₀(ETB) 0-9-6	' 8-5	7 7	G 12-7	W 0 6	g 12-0-7	w 11-0-6
8	FE₀(BS) 11-9-6	CAN 11-9-8	(12-8-5	8 8	H 12-8	X 0-7	h 12-0-8	x 11-0-7
9	FE₁(HT) 12-9-5	EM 11-9-8-1	) 11-8-5	9 9	I 12-9	Y 0-8	i 12-0-9	y 11-0-8
10	FE₂(LF) 0-9-5	SUB 9-8-7	* 11-8-4	: 8-2	J 11-1	Z 0-9	j 12-11-1	z 11-0-9
11	FE₃(VT) 12-9-8-3	ESC 0-9-7	+ 12-8-6	; 11-8-6	K 11-2	[Ä 12-8-2	k 12-11-2	{ ä 12-0
12	FE₄(FF) 12-9-8-4	IS₄(FS) 11-9-8-4	, 0-8-3	< 12-8-4	L 11-3	\ Ö 0 8-2	l 12-11-3	| ö 12-11
13	FE₅(CR) 12-9-8-5	IS₃(GS) 11-9-8-5	- 11	= 8-6	M 11 4	] Å 11-8-2	m 12-11-4	} å 11-0
14	SO 12-9-8-6	IS₂(RS) 11-9-8-6	. 12-8-3	> 0-8-6	N 11-5	^ Ü 11-8-7	n 12-11-5	¯ ü 11-0-1
15	SI 12-9-8-7	IS₁(US) 11-9-8-7	/ 0-1	? 0-8-7	O 11-6	_ 0-8-5	o 12-11-6	DEL 12-9-7

3

Fortran

Fortran may truly be said to be the grandfather of all high-level programming languages. It has been around for nearly 30 years and is still going strong.

I remember very well the time I first heard of it during my days at the Saab Aircraft Co. We were a few young people working with automatic coding as it was then called. The world was young and open for anybody to conquer.

I came into the room of a colleague and saw that something was amiss. He was rocking to and fro and pointing to a manual before him. It was entitled 'Formula Translation System — ForTran'. 'This is a knock-out', he said 'this is a knock-out. We have nothing more to do'.

My colleague evidently knew a success when he saw it. By recounting this little episode I want to stress how drastically Fortran changed things. The idea of standard programs was new. The idea of libraries was just appearing. Nobody had yet written about automatic formula translation. Yet here it was. The flood gates were open. Fortran was implemented on hundreds of systems. It became the language every scientific programmer had to know. Then came Algol, Basic, Cobol and a host of other languages. By the time Fortran was standardised by ANSI in 1966 and ISO in 1969 [1], it seemed already obsolete, ready to be swept away by progress. But enthusiasts on the American West Coast gave Fortran a second lease on life. In 1977, ANSI issued a new standard, commonly known as Fortran 77 [2]. This brought Fortran back into the mainstream of progress And the work goes on. Another major revision, nick-named Fortran 8X, is in the works. Now it seems likely that Fortran will survive into the next century.

Why was Fortran such a success? One answer is of course that it got there first. But the main reason is that it happened to strike the right balance between high-level and low-level; high-level enough to represent a big lift over all assembler languages, yet close enough to the machine to allow fast execution, and — very importantly — getting around the system. If you lacked something in Fortran you could write your own assembler subroutine. The interface was easy enough for any reasonably skilled programmer to do that. If you had to turn a dirty trick, Fortran was permissive enough to let you. A compiler writer could extend it almost indefinitely. So Fortran grew according to the computing world's needs. By now its position is well-nigh unshakeable.

The Fortran 66 standard is a committee's work after a host of implementations, and it shows. Important things were left out of the standard because it would have been impossible to agree. Sometimes it is downright inconsistent, as when it permits the user to write an end-of-file but gives him no way of sensing it on reading. (The END=label construct is actually not in the 66 standard.) Sometimes it is really quaint, as in the PAUSE statement which allows the user to display a maximum of five octal digits. All over the world, managers were telling programmers to stick to the Fortran standard. They literally did not know what they were talking about. The standard worked because implementors did not stick to it, but continued to extend it, sometimes copying other people's extensions, occasionally breaking new ground. One European manufacturer, needless to say without Fortran experience, did implement it to the letter. They say no compiler ever caused so many portability problems as that one.

Lest you mistake this for criticism, let me say at once that there is just one thing worse than a post-implementation standard, and that is a pre-implementation one. It is an academic construction, a straitjacket. You just can't think up a language, foresee all the uses it will be put to and make it practical for every such purpose without trying it out. (If the Ada people succeed at it, it will be a historical first.) And if you did produce a good language you would probably find it had some implementation snag that made it prohibitively inefficient. Even we Algol people, who used to take our Report as gospel, dropped a few little things like numeric labels and dynamic *own* arrays in implementation. No, it can't be done that way either. If you want a good, working standard you have to have a give-and-take between definition and implementation. The standards committee has to define a language and then go on working actively with the first batch of implementors, changing, adding to and interpreting the document, occasionally taking a bold stand that sends half the implementors back to the drawing board. Standards work is seldom done that way, but it ought to be.

A thorough analysis of the Fortran 66 standard revealed seven major areas where it was not sufficient to give portability. They are listed below and I shall discuss them in turn, concentrating on the ones that are still unsolved in Fortran 77. They are:

(1) There was no definition of word length and precision.
(2) String handling was very limited and quite non-standard.
(3) Special constructs were left undefined.
(4) There were no facilities for control of overflow and no error handling generally.
(5) No sensing of end-of-file and error condition in I/O.

(6) No direct access I/O.

(7) No definition of special I/O like paper tape and plotter.

An eighth problem area, non-standard facilities for overlaying large programs, belongs to the border area between Fortran and command language. It will be discussed briefly in the chapter on command languages.

Before starting the detailed discussion of these problem areas, let me give you a couple of references. Verifying that a program is completely within the standard can be done automatically, e.g. by Ryder's PFORT Verifier [3]. The many local dialects of Fortran have been thoroughly investigated by Muxworthy [4]. The reader is referred to these works for complete information on Fortran 66 portability.

3.1 WORD LENGTH AND PRECISION

Computers have very varying word lengths and varying schemes for real arithmetic. At various times the market has offered machines with integer word lengths ranging from 16 to 60 bits, precision ranging from 24 to 48 and exponent parts of 8 or 12 bits. In addition, there is usually a double precision facility with roughly double the number of bits for precision and, as often as not, a larger exponent range as well. Fortran 66 and 77 recognise the existence of two precisions, REAL and DOUBLE PRECISION. Both are undefined beyond the very minimum requirement that the precision of DOUBLE PRECISION be better than (not necessarily double!) that of REAL. Naturally, every implementation uses the built-in precisions of their respective machines. So when you port a program its arithmetic may become more or less precise according to circumstances. Similarly, a program that worked within the word length available for integers on machine 1 may break down after being ported to machine 2.

This problem might in principle be solved in any of three different ways:

(A) You might prescribe the meaning of REAL and DOUBLE PRECISION more strictly.

(B) You might supply the user with functions to find out the precision of the machine at hand.

(C) You might allow the user to request a certain degree of precision.

Method A is almost certainly not viable. Suppose we decided that henceforth REAL would mean 28 bits of precision and an 8 bit exponent. This would be fine for 36 bit machines, but what would an implementor do if he had a 32 bit machine? He would hardly implement all REALS as 64 bit words. If the implementor had a 48 bit machine he would not have that problem, but do you think his users would use DOUBLE PRECISION if they needed only 40 bit words? They would use REAL, knowing that it was sufficient in practice. It might have worked in the 1960s when 36 bits was on the point of being a *de facto* standard, but it would be doomed today.

Method B is fairly easy to implement, and in some cases it is also very useful. It is useful if you are controlling an iterative computation and need to know how small a tolerance it is realistic to set. In this case, you do not have a definite precision requirement. You are just trying to get the best results out of the machine actually at hand. You could also use it to plant a check at the beginning of the run, warning the user that on this machine the precision is too small and the program is likely to fail unless converted to double precision. That would leave some manual work to the user, but it would be an improvement on the present state of the art.

I used to believe in method C and tried to implement it, so by now I have a fair understanding of the problems connected with it. The idea is that you would be allowed to declare the precision you want. Instead of writing 'REAL X', you would be allowed to write, say, 'REAL * 10 X'. This would give you built-in single or double precision according to whether the single precision of the machine could handle 10 (decimal) digits of precision or not. This sounds simple, so simple indeed that I might be forgiven for believing that it could be handled by a pre-processor.

Not so. The first problem was that, under the 66 standard, format codes were tied to the precision of the variable being input or output. Therefore variable lists and formats had to be analysed carefully in order to match variables with formats. This is not always possible, since arrays in the variable list may be of a variable length, not known until run time. A second problem was the correspondence between actual and formal parameters in function and subroutine calls. If strict compatibility of word length was required, every Fortran subprogram would have to come in a dozen declared precisions (all of which would actually compile to either a real or double precision version). Another major problem for a pre-processor was implementation of EQUIVALENCE between variables of different precision. Finally we would have to look at the way this scheme would be used in practice. Would the user every time think over the precision requirements when he wrote the program? More likely he would quickly fall into the habit of using the two precisions that corresponded to those built into the machine. And if the user was energetic and declared 'REAL * 8 X', how was he to know that 8 digits were actually enough if the current machine gave him 10? The scheme would have to have a facility for actually destroying unwanted precision as a way of checking the precision requirement. After considering all of these questions, I reluctantly came to the conclusion that this could not be done, at least not by pre-compiler.

Fortran 77 adopted none of the schemes described above. Quietly, however, great progress was made by making the implicit functions generic, i.e. functions which took on the types of their parameters. Thus the same function name can always be used for the function. Similarly, format codes became interchangeable. In Fortran 77 it is allowed to use the E format code with a double precision variable. Under these rules it is no longer necessary to go through the whole program to change the precision. It is enough to change the declarations at the beginning of the program and add declarations for implicitly typed variables.

Both methods B and C are being added to Fortran 8X, so we shall presently come back to these questions again.

3.2 STRING HANDLING

The string handling of Fortran 66 was rudimentary indeed. You could handle variables (of other declared types) as 'Hollerith' variables. All you could do with these under the standard was to assign a Hollerith constant value to the variable or input a value to it, and then reproduce that value on output. This construction was the after-effect of regarding strings as essentially texts to garnish numerical results. But times changed and requirements grew. A number of schemes, for example, the well-known ENCODE–DECODE, sprang up to handle parts of strings, to compare them, concatenate them and convert them to and from numbers. In due time string handling was incorporated in the 77 standard. It includes the new data type CHARACTER; conversion between strings and numbers is handled by variations of READ and WRITE.

```
IRON = 'Fe'
READ (11, '(A)') MATRL
IF (MATRL.EQ.IRON) THEN
  . . .
```

One problem remained: the collating sequence. We have mentioned this briefly under Data Representation. Now let us go into it thoroughly. The collating sequence, as we have said, defines the manner in which the computer orders characters and hence strings. The bit representation of the characters used defines the 'native' collating sequence, the one the system will use unless otherwise ordered. The problem is that they are different from system to system.

Fortran 77 includes comparisons between strings with the operators .EQ., .GT., etc. But comparison with .GT. turns out differently between the same strings depending on the machine: it may be that '2' .GT. 'a' is true on one machine and false on another. All the standard prescribes is that the digits zero to nine should be ordered correctly among themselves, the letters A to Z likewise, and that blank should collate below either of these series.

Now it is not very expensive to introduce a comparison function that works the same way on all systems and compares according to the ASCII collating sequence. You do not even have to convert all the characters to ASCII to do it; all you have to convert is the first pair of characters that are unequal. If you compare the strings 'REAL' and 'R2-D2' all you need to know is whether 'E' is greater or less than '2'. That settles it. Such a comparison function will come in Fortran 8X as it already has in modern Cobol and a number of other languages.

I used to be very strict in this matter of string comparison until one day in 1979 when I was listening to a colleague lecturing at an ISPRA software course on portability. He was advocating strict ASCII sorting, and I was nodding approval: this tallied with my ideas. Suddenly Bill Waite of Colorado State spoke up and said: 'Show me an example where it matters!'

The lecturer and I tore into him. We repeated all the arguments already advanced and asserted that there could be no true portability without a well-defined collating sequence.

'Right', said Waite, 'but show me an example where it matters!'

We could not, try as we might. The incident started me thinking. Waite certainly had a point. As long as the collating sequence was reasonable in the sense that it conformed to the minimum required by Fortran 77, it often did not matter what it was. In the typical two file merge, for instance, it is immaterial how a file is sorted, because the program that retrieves the information will use the same collating sequence as the one that sorted it. The retrieval program will be independent of the collating sequence. All you have to think of is to re-sort the file if you want to port it. Again, if you have a program where all the string compares are with .EQ. or .NE. but not with .GT. and .LT., it will work in the same manner regardless of the collating sequence. I would still vote for a standard collating sequence because it removes all these problems at a marginal cost, but do not be too unhappy if you cannot have it right away.

There is a further point about sorting which mainly concerns languages other than English. If you sort for output that is to be published, you will often have to devise your own collating sequence, or even collating algorithm. Few national ASCII codes correspond exactly to their alphabets. If you publish, say, an address list, you will also often want to have special sorting rules. You will almost certainly wish to have small and capital letters have the same value, except if the only difference between two words is one of case. Similarly, you may want to lump all characters that are not letters or digits — hyphens, full stops, ampersands and what have you — into the same value. The Swedish directory inserts full stops between capital letters that appear in sequence and therefore are regarded as abbreviations; thus 'ISO' would collate as 'I.S.O.'. In such applications the ASCII and the native collating sequence become unimportant.

3.3 SPECIAL CONSTRUCTS

Under this heading we find some constructs well known to old Fortran hands. There is the 'zero trip loop', i.e. the case when the controlled variable of a loop has already passed the final value when the loop is entered, as in

DO 100 I = 1,N

when N happens to be zero. On some systems this would cause one execution of the loop, on other systems none. The 66 standard left the effect undefined.

This is the right place to discuss the meaning of that often abused word 'undefined'. Most programming language definitions, starting, I think, with the Algol 60 Report, either do not define the effect of certain constructs or situations, or explicitly declare them to be undefined. There is no real distinction between explicit and implicit undefinition. They both mean that the standard does not say what the construct means or what happens in the situation in question. It is not an error, it is outside the standard. In the case of the DO loop, the implementor is free to do as he chooses: he may have the system execute the loop once, skip the loop or abort the program with an error message, or, for that matter, without a message. An ambitious implementor might even give the user a compiler option to control the interpretation of the undefined case.

The same situation exists if a statement begins with a keyword unknown to the standard. So, you see, these definitions can be very permissive. This is sometimes expressed by the aphorism: 'One man's error is another man's extension'. As you will see from the next section, I am not particularly fond of this way of interpreting standards, but that's how it is.

The 77 standard interpreted the zero loop construct to mean that the loop should be skipped. This was a bold move, considering that the one-execution interpretation was the more prevalent one, though obviously less logical.

Another troublesome construct is the out-of-bounds computed GO TO, e.g. the case:

GO TO (10, 20, 30) N

with N zero or greater than 3. Formerly undefined, this situation now means the next statement in sequence is executed.

3.4 EXCEPTION HANDLING

As I have just stated, Fortran 66 does not prescribe a way of handling situations that are outside the standard. So if you get overflow and wrong result adding two large numbers, your system will not necessarily complain. Also, there is no way within the standard of finding out: the facilities for jumping on overflow that exist in several implementations, and in other languages like PL/I, are not in the Fortran 66 standard. The Fortran 77 standard is no improvement in this respect.

To illustrate how bad the situation is, let me show you the following example:

```
INTEGER K, L
K = 5000000
L = K * K
PRINT L
END
```

It is an interesting exercise to run this on four different machines:

— Machine A (24 bits word length) signals a compile-time error (the constant 5000000 is too large for this machine).
— Machine B (32 bits) gives a run-time abort (overflow).
— Machine C (36 bits) gives a wrong result without warning (integer overflow is not trapped).
— Machine D (48 bits) gives the right result (believe it or not!).

In a more mature branch of technology this sort of thing would be regarded as unacceptable; and let us realise that we cannot go on forever basing computations that result in highway bridges and moon rockets on such loose foundations.

A minimum requirement for an industrial standard is that it should be possible to sense errors, and that unsensed errors should at least give a warning output.

I shall come back to this question of exception handling further on. For the moment, let us just be content with having given a picture of the situation. It is of course not quite so bad in practice, since usually there are facilities for over-flow handling, similar from system to system.

3.5 END-OF-FILE AND ERROR CONDITIONS IN I/O

This was a serious gap in the 66 standard. It is most inconvenient to have a program aborted because the input file is read to the end; in fact that is usually when the real fun should begin. Similarly, we can't have the program abort every time there is an error in the input records. Yet, in the absence of facilities for handling these cases, this is just what a conscientious implementor might do.

This problem is now solved, since the 77 standard included the END=label and ERR=label constructs in the READ statement in the manner that had long been a *de facto* standard.

3.6 DIRECT ACCESS I/O

Again, here was a gap in the 66 standard, though it did not affect almost every program in the way the lack of end-of-file and error sensing did. Again, there existed a *de facto* standard for direct access I/O. It required the user to define a file by a DEFINE statement, and then allowed him to write and read using special variations of the ordinary I/O statements.

In this case, Fortran 77 broke new ground. The direct access I/O became a special case of the new I/O system. This system allows file operations at program language level which were formerly only available at command language level. Moreover, it is the first time such file operations are standardised. I shall therefore describe it in some detail.

It includes the statements OPEN, CLOSE and INQUIRE with the following syntax: (default keywords in italics)

OPEN (UNIT=u, IOSTAT=ios, ERR=s, FILE=fin, STATUS=sta,
ACCESS=acc, FORM=fm, RECL=rl, BLANK=blnk)

UNIT=u	u is the unit number (this is the only mandatory specifier).
IOSTAT=ios	ios receives a zero if the OPEN went well, and a positive, implementation-dependent number otherwise.
ERR=s	s is an error label.
FILE=fin	fin is a file name.
STATUS=sta	sta can have the values OLD, NEW, SCRATCH, or *UNKNOWN*, and gives the status of the file.
ACCESS=acc	acc takes the values *SEQUENTIAL* or DIRECT, and thus specifies the access to the file.
FORM=fm	fm takes the values *FORMATTED* or UNFORMATTED.
RECL=rl	rl specifies the record length for a direct access file. Note that the value of rl is processor-dependent for an UNFORMATTED file.
BLANK=blnk	blnk can have the values *NULL* or ZERO, and controls the interpretation of blanks in numeric input.

CLOSE (UNIT=u, IOSTAT=ios, ERR=s, STATUS=sta)

CLOSE has the same specifiers as OPEN, except that sta here takes the value KEEP or DELETE and controls the continued existence or not of the file after the run. The default is DELETE for SCRATCH files, and KEEP otherwise.

INQUIRE (UNIT=u, other_specifiers)   or
INQUIRE (FILE=fin, other_specifiers)

where other_specifiers are:

IOSTAT=ios, ERR=s, EXIST=ex, OPENED=od, NUMBER=num,

NAMED=nmd, NAME=fn, ACCESS=acc, SEQUENTIAL=seq, DIRECT=dir, FORM=fm, FORMATTED=fmt, UNFORMATTED=unf, RECL=rl, NEXTREC=nr, BLANK=blnk

Thus you can inquire by unit or by file name and INQUIRE will return values to any of the other specifiers you have asked for. You can find out, in turn, if the file is at the moment in an error condition (and jump to s if it is), whether the file exists, whether it is connected to a unit, to which unit it is connected (num), if it has a name and which one, the access method, the formatting, the record length, the position of a direct access file, and the blank interpretation.

The three statements OPEN, CLOSE and INQUIRE can, together with the old READ, WRITE and ENDFILE do much of what is needed in the way of file handling: create, modify and delete files. We shall discuss in the command language chapter what extra facilities might be needed.

3.7 SPECIAL I/O

Here we are on the borderline between programming language and command language. I shall discuss the problem in the particular context of graphics standards. Paper tape I/O, etc., can be handled in a similar way.

When I first considered this question, standards work on graphics had barely started. It seemed that the set of routines originally written by Calcomp for their plotters was the nearest thing to a *de facto* standard. A new standard for graphics seemed a long way off, and people worried, among other things, about whether there would have to be a graphics annex to each programming language. In 1976, standards work started with a conference at Seillac, and by late 1981 the Windsor meeting of ISO TC97/SC5, which handles programming languages, adopted the GKS standard for processing as a draft proposal [5]. This standard defines about one hundred functions covering everything from simple plotting to advanced, multi-station graphics input. The standard describes functions and parameters in a general manner that can be adapted to any programming language. Moreover, an annex to the standard defines a *metafile,* i.e. a way of describing a picture in the form of coordinate polygons, rasters and texts etc., on a file.

This allows the implementor to completely separate the software for generating a metafile from the software for drawing the picture defined by the file. The generating software can be application-dependent only and completely machine-independent and portable. The drawing software is, by contrast, the same for all pictures and depends only on the machine system and the device. This is a very useful idea, applicable in areas far removed from graphics. In fact, I doubt if the GKS committee saw all the implications of this idea, or they would not have put it in an annex. They would have made the metafile description the standard, and the one hundred functions the annex.

Let us recapitulate the effect of Fortran 77 on the seven problem areas identified in Fortran 66.

(1) The precision problem was eased considerably.
(2) The string handling problem was solved except for strict collating.
(3) The effects of the special constructs were defined.
(4) Exception handling – no change.
(5) EOF and errors in I/O – solved.
(6) Direct access I/O – solved.
(7) Special I/O – solved by other means.

Speaking loosely, we might say two-thirds of the portability problems were solved.

Many other improvements came with Fortran 77 that have not yet been mentioned, since they have no direct bearing on portability. Let us mention the following:

— The IF-THEN-ELSE construct.
— List directed I/O. No explicit format specification is required. The form of external representation is determined by the list item.
— Mixed type expressions.
— Compile-time constants.
— Implicit type declarations.
— Array bounds: both upper and lower bounds may be declared. Up to seven dimensions are allowed.
— A character string may be used as a format directly in the I/O statement.
— A character array may be used as an internal file.
— Values of entities in subprograms may be SAVEd between calls.
— An asterisk may be used instead of C in column 1 to designate a comment.

The IF-THEN-ELSE constructs allows the writing of conditional statements without GO TOs. The complete construct is:

IF (condition-1) THEN
statements to be executed if condition-1 holds
ELSE IF (condition-2) THEN
statements to be executed if condition-2 (but not -1) holds
. . .
ELSE
statements to be executed if none of the specified conditions hold
END IF

The ELSE IF and ELSE clauses are optional. This feature opened the possibility of structured programming in Fortran.

I will intentionally avoid a complete description of the many other facilities of Fortran 77, since it is already available through all major manufacturers. So this list, along with the facilities described earlier in the chapter, are just meant to stimulate your interest. If you have not yet read about Fortran 77, do adopt it as the next item on your reading list. If you are an active Fortran 66 programmer, there is no better way to spend the next weekend. You would recoup the time many times over.

3.8 FORTRAN 8X

The ANS committee X3J3 that developed Fortran 77 continues its work with the intent of producing a new Fortran standard (here called Fortran 8X). The work is carried on in cooperation with a European expert group. The current status of the work is summarised below, with attention focussed on the remaining portability problems and on important improvements, the latter forming a background for our discussion of better programming languages in the last chapter of this book. Readers with knowledge of other programming languages will recognise ideas from PL/I, APL, Algol, Pascal, etc.

The summary is a condensation of the committee's standing document S6.86 [6] which consists of all proposals (provisionally) accepted by X3J3 up to May 1983. The numbering of S6.86 is used here. The features are mainly introduced through simple examples. Comments within the code are preceded by exclamation marks (!) in accordance with Fortran 8X program form.

#1 Improved control structures

A new DO-loop and a CASE construct have been accepted; these are important enhancements though not in the order of IF-THEN-ELSE.

(a) The new DO-loop has the format

DO (control)

. . .

REPEAT

In this modernised DO-loop, 'control' can be as now, e.g. I=1,N but there are also new facilities, e.g. N TIMES.
No (control) gives an infinite loop.
DO-loops can be named, and exited by 'EXIT name'.

DO (I=1,N)

. . .

IF(CH(I:I).EQ.' ') EXIT   ! name omitted if DO not nested

. . .

REPEAT

(b) The CASE construct consists of a SELECT statement specifying the variable on which selection is to be made; one or more CASE statements, each followed by statements to be executed if the variable is within the range of that CASE; an optional DEFAULT case; an END SELECT.

    The CASE construct allows the user to choose one of several alternatives according to the value of a variable. Compact ways are given to describe the ranges within which the variables should lie for a branch to be taken. If the variable is in no defined range, the default case will be taken.

```
INTEGER FUNCTION SIGNUM(N)    ! Signum takes the value
                              ! -1, 0 or 1,
SELECT CASE(N)                ! according as N is
CASE(:-1)                     ! negative
     SIGNUM=-1
```

```
      CASE(0)                    ! zero
         SIGNUM=0
      CASE(1:)                   ! or positive
         SIGNUM=1
      END SELECT
      END
```

#2 Data structures

There is now a proposal for data structures for Fortran 8X, modelled on Pascal. It works in the following manner.

A data structure is declared in two steps. The first step is to define the structure, in effect creating a new type. The second step is to declare variables (or as they are sometimes called, instances) of the new type. The examples below show the definition and declaration of variables of the new types ID and PERSON:

(a) Definition of a structure	FORM ID CHARACTER L*30, F*20 END FORM ID
(b) Declaration	ID: ANAME, BNAME
(c) Structure within a structure	FORM PERSON ID: NAME INTEGER PNR CHARACTER*25 BIRTHPLACE LOGICAL SEX END FORM PERSON
Declaration of persons	PERSON: PA, MA
(d) Reference to a field a structure	MA.PNR = 3001093529 IF (PA.EQ.MA) THEN

As you can see, once a variable of a structured type has been declared, one can refer to the whole variable or part of it, called a field.

In the case of Fortran, there is a slight catch about using the full stop to separate a structure name from a field name. The full stop is already used to delimit some operators. If the last example is considered by itself, it is not immediately obvious whether PA.EQ.MA is the subfield MA of the field EQ of the structured variable PA, or whether the .EQ. is the equals operator.

Structured constants are easy to define: The whole of MA can be assigned to by:

MA = (('SMITH','MARGARET'),3001093925,'LONDON',.FALSE.)

Recently the proposal has been expanded to allow variant structures. This means a part of the structure can differ from instance to instance, according to the value of a so-called tag field. This tag field must be part of the structure and belong to its fixed part which precedes the variable part. This facility corresponds to the mixing of different record types in a file, which is allowed in Cobol.

#3 Array Processing

This is one of the heaviest sections of the whole Fortran 8X proposal and a detailed description would be outside the scope of this book. The salient parts are the following.

(1) Functions can have array results. This applies both to user defined functions and new intrinsic functions. Many new intrinsic functions are defined for array operations: matrix multiplication and division, inversion, transpose, sum, product, shifts, etc.

(2) Arrays can be used as operands and as function arguments where Fortran 77 only accepts simple variables. If one operand (argument) is an array, the other operands (arguments) have to be arrays of the same shape or scalars; the scalars being expanded to arrays of the same shape. For example, assuming A, B and C are arrays, the following statements are allowed:

```
A = 0.0      ! All elements of A become zero
A = B+C      ! A becomes the sum of arrays B and C
A = A−1.0    ! All elements of A are decreased by 1.0
A = SIN(B)   ! Each element of A becomes the sine of the corresponding
             ! element of B
```

Not all functions can be treated this way. The ones that can are called 'elemental', and these are essentially functions of simple variables giving simple results, like the elementary functions. A function which in its base version has one or more array arguments will be called 'transformational' and cannot be used in this way.

(3) The rank, size and bounds of an array can be found as a function of the array name. Therefore it will not be necessary to supply the bounds of an array along with its name as arguments to a procedure; the bounds can be omitted since they can be retrieved from within the procedure. This facility was introduced quite recently. Since it is in any case necessary in order to implement the many intrinsic array functions, making it available to the user was a logical step that cost nothing extra.

(4) An array constant, called 'array constructor' has been introduced. As an example, consider the following assignment of the lengths of the months of the year to the array MONLEN:

MONLEN = (31,28,31,30,31,30,2(31),30,31,30,31)

(The proposal text has square brackets here; I hope it is an oversight since square brackets collide with the national letters!)

(5) Arrays will be much more dynamic than before. One can write:

ALLOCATE (A(N), B(N,M))

and thus create arrays with bounds that vary from execution to execution of the program. This is a most important contribution to getting safe and economical programs.

Arrays that have been ALLOCATEd can be FREEd, releasing the storage occupied for other uses.

(6) There are several facilities for accessing parts of arrays, e.g. A(*,2) means the second column of A (array sections). The most general of these facilities is the IDENTIFY statement which resembles the old statement function:

IDENTIFY ⟨N⟩ DIAGA(I) = A(I,I) ! DIAGA is the diagonal of A
IDENTIFY ⟨N,M/2⟩ EV2B(I,J) = B(I,2*J)
    ! EV2B is formed by the even-numbered columns of B
    ! Quantities in ⟨⟩ are subscript bounds

(7) There is a WHERE-OTHERWISE construct which is a sort of super IF statement. Example:

```
LOGICAL L(10,10)
REAL A(10,10), B(10,10), C(10,10)
. . .
WHERE (A.GT.B)
A = B
C = 1
OTHERWISE
C = 0
ENDWHERE
. . .
WHERE (L) A = 0
```

(The whole array proposal is still in a state of flux. It contains some recently introduced contradictions concerning points 3 and 5. Point 3 restricts the use of the rank and bounds finding functions for assumed size arrays, though this is precisely the important use for those functions; there is a contradiction between point 5 and #7 on whether allocatable arrays can appear in the main program. In both cases I have interpreted the text in favor of greater generality because there seems to be no implementation difficulty attached to doing so. No doubt these matters will be cleared up shortly.)

#4 'Enhanced subroutine calls'
Several proposals have been adopted to enhance subroutine calls.

(1) One can give the parameters of the call in a different order than the declared one by prefixing each parameter with a keyword. The names of the formal parameters in the called procedure are used as keywords. (This means the compiler must know a bit about the called procedure, and thus seems to be a break with Fortran's tradition of independent compilation of different program units. We shall return to this matter in due course.) One can also declare keywords in the calling program unit, if one does not like the default keywords, or if the called procedure is a formal parameter and thus unknown at compile time.

An actual argument without a keyword (as is normal today) is associated with the dummy argument immediately following the most recently associated dummy argument. If the actual argument is the first in the call, it is of course associated with the first dummy argument.

(2) A parameter may be left out, if it was declared OPTIONAL. One can, from inside the procedure, find out whether or not it exists by using the function PRESENT ( ).

Example: Let the procedure declaration be

    SUBROUTINE P(A,B,C)
    OPTIONAL B
    IF(.NOT.PRESENT(B)) B = −1.
    . . .

The calls P(A,C=2.5) and P(A,,2.5) will be equivalent and legal; the first statement of the program will be executed and give B the default value −1.

3. One can define the 'direction' of a formal parameter by the declaration INTENT and the attributes IN or OUT or both.

If the parameter is an IN parameter, the procedure will read from it. The parameter must therefore be defined before procedure entry.

 If the parameter is an OUT parameter, the procedure will write in it. The parameter must be a variable or an array element, not a constant or an expression.

#5 Program form

#5.1 *Free format*

Under this heading there are a number of changes that will modernise Fortran's program form and make it easier to input programs from a terminal. I am not particularly fond of them, program form being one of the things that make you feel at home in your old language, and it has to be mentioned that two of them are going to prevent the use of old programs without a conversion (which can be done automatically, however).

(a) Statements need not begin in column 7, and specifically they can begin in column 1, colliding with the old comment form.
(b) Continuation is signalled by one ampersand (&) at the end of the old line and one at the beginning of the new line.

#5.2 *'Significant blanks'*

Blanks will separate words from each other, and thus can be used, for example, to separate keywords from identifiers. This proposal was accepted by a hair's breadth after a long and interesting debate, where the major arguments were:

Pro:
The Fortran language was becoming overloaded with separators and too context-dependent. For instance, if 'DO 13 K=1,5' was misspelt 'DO 13 K=1.5', it would be interpreted as the assignment 'DO13K = 1.5'. (This particular bug is said to have crashed a moon shot!) Natural language has significant blanks and we tend to think of blanks as delimiting words.

Con:
Old programs would have to be converted if their blanks were squeezed out or if there were blanks inserted into identifiers and numbers.

Significant blanks have not yet been used consistently in Fortran 8X syntax. For instance, the parentheses around control in the new DO, or the colon after a form identifier are now superfluous. The full stops surrounding EQ, LT etc. are also superfluous and could be phased out in the long run, leaving the full stop free for its use as decimal point and field separator.

#5.3 *Longer identifiers*
Identifiers may contain up to 31 characters, including the underline character ( ).
Example: NO_OF_RECORDS.

#6 **Precision data type**

#6.1 *Controlled Precision*
The facility of being able to request the precision to suit the problem has been discussed extensively. There have been considerable difficulties finding a facility which is non-trivial without being unduly expensive and complicated.

The preliminary proposal includes declarations like:

REAL (PRECISION_10=8,EXP_RANGE=30) X,Y,Z

which make the compiler choose between the local computer's REAL and DOUBLE PRECISION types for the variables. (PRECISION_10 and EXP_RANGE are keywords that can be left out if the parameters are given in the order above.) A similar facility works for the type COMPLEX (but not for INTEGER).

Constants in such a declared precision are signalled by the use of an exponent character other than D or E, which is declared:

REAL_CHARACTER (8,30) H

which then allows you to write, for example:

X = 3.1415926H0

Arithmetic operations between variables of different type are performed using the precision and range of the most demanding variable.

Assignment is done after converting the expression to the type of the receiving variable.

For procedure calls there usually has to be an exact type match between the actual and formal parameters. If one, however, has specified one or more parameters and the function value to be GENERIC, one can make the function value take on the type of the parameter(s), the way it is done for example, in the Fortran 77 SIN function, which would have the specification:

GENERIC (REAL, DOUBLE PRECISION) SIN, X

In many cases, the same procedure body may be used unchanged for different parameter types, since the arithmetic operators, the assignment operator (=) and many intrinsic functions are generic and thus adapt automatically to the types of the parameters.

A number of procedures for 'Environment Enquiries' have been accepted after being requested by groups which work with procedure libraries; with those one can find out the number system, number range and precision of the current computer. It is assumed that integers can be described in terms of a base r and a number of digits q. Similarly reals can be described in terms of an exponent part $s*b**e$ and a fractional part with the base b and p digits. The procedures that find out what properties the current computer has are seven:

RADIX(X)   returns r if X is integer, and b if X is real.
PRECISION(X)   q for integers, p for reals
MINEXP(X)   the smallest permitted value of e
MAXEXP(X)   the largest permitted value of e
HUGE(X)   largest positive number of same type as X

| TINY(X) | smallest positive number of same type as X |
| EPSILON(X) | the smallest number such that 1+EPSILON(X) of same type as X can be distinguished from 1. |

On a certain machine, each of these functions has one constant value for all real X and another one for all integer X. They are of interest when the same program is widely distributed and a facility is needed to find out its current environment.

In addition, there are several procedures for handling numbers, for example, EXPONENT(X) returns the value of the exponent e for the current x.

#7 Recursive procedures

Rather unexpectedly, recursive procedures have been accepted. The recursive property is specified by preceding SUBROUTINE or 'type FUNCTION' by the word RECURSIVE. Such a procedure may be called recursively (ordinary procedures may not). Each recursive call creates a new instance of the procedure with its own set of local variables. An entity that is SAVEd is however not replicated; the same entity is accessible from all instances of the procedure.

#8 The BIT data type

A BIT data type has been introduced with the following properties:

(a) It is declared e.g. BIT BYTE*8, LOGMAT*1(100,100)
(b) Operators // .BNOT. .BAND. .BOR. .... .EQ. .NE. are available. One has changed .NOT. to .BNOT. and so on in order to distinguish operations on BIT entities from operations on LOGICAL.
(c) Procedures for shift, conversion, assignment, etc. are defined.
(d) Some kind of I/O for binary tapes is being discussed.

#9 Procedure interaction

#9.1 *Internal procedures*

A program unit can contain local subroutines and functions, which are specified INTERNAL. Internal procedures replace statement functions. A very interesting innovation is that an internal procedure can also create a new operator, or extend the meaning of an old operator (the 'over-loading' concept, known from Algol 68 and Ada). For instance, one could assign a meaning to plus between logical variables by the declaration:

```
LOGICAL INTERNAL FUNCTION LPLUS(A,B) OPERATOR +
LOGICAL LA,LB
LPLUS = LA.NEQ.LB
```

#9.2 *Shared data*

COMMON and BLOCK DATA are replaced by more general and easier-to-use mechanisms, USE and BUNDLE.

USE allows the user to specify the use in one program unit or internal procedure of entities known in another program unit or the host procedure. One need not, as in COMMON, declare all variables in the common area, but only those actually used. Thus, any of the following three USE statements might be used instead of the COMMON statement below them:

```
USE / GDR / ALL
USE / GDR / ONLY (XMIN,XMAX,YMIN,YMAX)
USE / GDR / EXCEPT (XOR,XSIZE,XSTEP,XC,YOR,YSIZE,YSTEP,YC)

COMMON / GDR / XMIN,XMAX,XOR,XSTEP,XC,
&                     YMIN,YMAX, YOR,YSIZE,YSTEP,YC
```

BUNDLE replaces BLOCK DATA but has a much wider use. It can include form definitions, variable declarations and procedures. A BUNDLE cannot be directly executed but only USEd from other program units. It is typically intended for program packages with common variables. A BUNDLE is considered active as long as there is any executing program unit directing a USE towards it, so if it is USEd from the main program its variables will stay defined throughout the whole program execution. Variables and procedures in the bundle can be protected from direct outside use by declaring them PRIVATE.

#10 Input/output
Again, there is a wealth of new features, the ones of most general interest being:

(a) Alphanumeric data for list input need not be surrounded by apostrophes in certain cases when they do not contain blanks and cannot be confused with numbers. (But list output still always produces unapostrophed output, and is not in general rereadable.)

(b) Name-directed I/O has been accepted.

Name-directed I/O goes into effect when the format is specified as double asterisk (**). The input may be for instance:

ICODE=4711, C=2.72,3.14,3*0.0, TYPES=REAL, 'DOUBLE
    PRECISION' /   and it is read by a program sequence like
REAL C(5)
CHARACTER TYPES*16(2)
. . .
READ(11,**) C, TYPES, ICODE, JCODE

The effect of the READ is to fill ICODE with 4711, C with 2.72, 3.14, 0.0, 0.0, 0.0, TYPES WITH 'REAL', 'DOUBLE PRECISION' (excluding the quotes), and leave JCODE unchanged. A later WRITE with the same list would reproduce the input, reordered according to the list. The value that happens to be in JCODE will also be output, preceded by JCODE=.

#11 Compile time facilities

(1) There is a new USING statement used to specify the use of a module or library.

```
USING GRAPHMOD  ! Use the graphics module
USING * PROCLIB=MY_LIB, PROCLIB=DEPT_LIB ! Search MY_LIB
        ! and DEPT_LIB, in that order, for needed procedures.
```

(2) There are compile time variables which can be used to control conditional complilation of program sequences.
(3) There has been extensive discussion of a macro facility. The following examples are from one of the proposals before the committee.
Example of a macro definition:

```
MACRO PERFORM(⟨TASK⟩) FOR ⟨BOUNDS⟩: OF ⟨VALUES⟩
DO (I = ⟨BOUNDS⟩)
IF (⟨VALUES⟩(I) .NE. 0) THEN
CALL ⟨TASK⟩(⟨VALUES⟩(I))
END IF
REPEAT
END MACRO PERFORM
```

Entities within ⟨⟩ are the formal parameters of the macro. As this shows, the call can be described quite freely; here parentheses, colon and the words FOR and OF are used. The macro calls a subroutine for a number of non-zero array elements.

Example of macro call:

    PERFORM (ADJUST) FOR J−1,J+10: OF WEIGHTS

The expanded program text:

    DO (I=J−1,J+10)
    IF (WEIGHTS(I) .NE. 0) THEN
    CALL ADJUST(WEIGHTS(I))
    END IF
    REPEAT

Macros are considered to give better language extension possibilities than can be had by introducing new subroutines and functions.

So far only parameterless macros have been accepted. Macros with parameters may or may not survive until the final proposal.

#12 Exception Handling

What is proposed here is a mechanism resembling the one used, I believe, in PL/I. It consists of four components:

(1) A method to specify the events that can be monitored (EVENTMARKs).

(2) A method to describe the processor's possible 'reactions' to events (HANDLERs).

(3) A method to connect a handler with an eventmark.

(4) A method to instruct the processor whether or not to monitor the events specified (ACTIVATE/DEACTIVATE).

This is another one of the recently introduced facilities, and currently examples of its application are lacking in the S6.86 text. A discussion of this and alternative mechanisms will come later. As we said earlier, we need facilities to handle errors like overflow and underflow, subscripts out of bounds, wrongly matched parameters, I/O errors, etc. One wants to be able to detect and act on errors and have a choice of making a jump, calling a procedure, or aborting the execution. Errors not taken care of by the programmer should give a warning.

#13 String handling

After evaluating the Fortran 77 CHARACTER type one now introduces strings of variable length (within a declared maximum length) plus a number of small enhancements like:

— Zero length strings.
— Functions to convert between a local code and ASCII.
— Substring of string constants.

#14 'Core and modules'

The idea is that Fortran 8X is to consist of a core with surrounding modules. The core shall be a complete, modern high level language.

Criteria for the core language are that it should be general purpose, portable, safe, efficient, concise and consistent, contemporary and upwards compatible.

The modules are BUNDLE units that provide end-user facilities. They are defined in terms of the core language, but standardised modules may be implemented more efficiently by implementors using assembler language and special hardware.

Sample modules could be Real Time Fortran, Data Base module and Graphics Module. The British have been working on a 'Conformity Module' giving strict rules on how to treat errors and prevent extensions; this is intended for use when portability is a prime consideration. I note with some regret that this has not been accepted in the current proposal.

The use of modules is specified by the command USING ⟨module name⟩ (see 11 above).

Fortran 8X will also contain features from Fortran 77 that are classified as deprecated or obsolete. These are elements that are to be phased out but not deleted until the next version of the standard (if then!) Candidates for this 'Obsolete Module' are:

— The old program form
— EQUIVALENCE statement
— COMMON statement and BLOCK DATA program unit
— passing an array element or substring to an array
— arithmetic IF statement
— computed GO TO statement
— alternate RETURN

- ASSIGN and assigned GO TO statements
- statement functions
- DOUBLE PRECISION
- specific names for intrinsic functions
- ENTRY statement
- DATA statement
- Fortran 77 DO statement
- DIMENSION statement
- PAUSE statement.

#15 Implicit none
Suppresses the automatic declaration and typing of variables.

As we see from the above, X3J3:s work covers a wide area. Those portability problems that were left unsolved in Fortran 77 are now being tackled, and many other matters besides. The only problem areas not being dealt with seem to be segmentation of large programs and a philosophy for interfacing with the operating system, which ought to be possible now that the work on common command language is in full swing.

In fact, the main problem with the work as many users see it, is that Fortran will be changed so much that manufacturers and users will feel a break in continuity. It is, however, an unquestionable advantage for all users that are tied to Fortran that modern facilities successively find their way into that language.

3.9 REFERENCES

[1] ISO 1539–1966; Programming Language Fortran.
[2] ISO 1539–1978; Information Processing – Programming Language Fortran.
[3] B. G. Ryder, Bell Laboratories; The PFORT Verifier; Software – Practice and Experience, Vol. 4, p. 359; 1974.
[4] D. T. Muxworthy, University of Edinburgh; A Review of Program Portability and Fortran Conventions; Report no. 1, European Computer Program Institute; 1976.
[5] ISO/DP 7942–1982; Information Processing – Graphical Kernel System (GKS) – Functional Description.
[6] ANS X3J3, Proposals Accepted for Future Fortran; Standing Document S6.86; May 1983 edition.

4

Command languages

4.1 INTRODUCTION

In this chapter we come to an area where standardisation has only recently begun, that of command languages.

Command languages are relative newcomers in data processing. In the early days there were no command languages. What had to be done to run a program, like starting it or mounting tapes was done by pressing buttons or by instructing operators — orally or in writing. In the early sixties, the first steps were taken to run a batch of jobs without manual intervention between each job. Instructions had to be replaced by 'control cards' — and command languages, also called job control languages or JCL, were born. They were used to assign tapes and call for compilations and runs. Some kind of user identification was needed for accounting purposes. A special card was used to set a time limit to the run, lest the job run on infinitely if caught in a loop.

With the advent of multiprocessing computers, command languages grew rapidly and developed new functions like reserving resources and calling for priority. New control cards were added when the need was felt to protect users from accessing one another's data. Out of this headlong and largely unplanned growth emerged a group of languages that hid their underlying similarity of purpose and functions under a bewildering variety of difficult syntax and semantics.

What they have in common is the following: the basic entity of the command language is the batch job (normally divided into job steps) or the interactive session; data are organised in files, that can be saved from job to job; activities in the job are initiated by commands that can compile and execute a program and perform different operations on files; program text and data can be included in the job besides the commands. On the other hand, there are great dissimilarities between the languages, functionally as well as syntactically: the attributes that can be given to files, like record lengths and block lengths, vary a great deal; the means of organising program files into libraries, and the intermediate stages of compilation are different. Most manufacturers' command languages have an undeveloped syntax and are difficult to learn and to use. A few (Burroughs, ICL) have however developed good, high level command languages.

4.2 THE DEVELOPMENT OF COMMAND LANGUAGE RESEARCH

4.2.1 Early Efforts and the Frostavallen Conference

The situation in command languages around 1970 was chaotic. For once, even

71

the optimists were hard put to see a bright future, which in this context would mean clean, portable command languages. The road we had to travel to today's situation, when that goal actually seems within reach, was long and arduous. Several new concepts had to be formed and integrated. I shall therefore invite you to retrace that road step by step, rather than take it all in one leap. It will of necessity be a somewhat personal account; other people will have been exposed to roughly the same ideas, but in a different sequence and from different sources.

My personal reaction to the command language situation was no different from that of most people from the pioneer days. We were shocked by the red tape that had now become necessary to run a job. We learned as little about the mess as we had to in order to run our jobs and hoped the problem would go away. I remember arguing against command language work at a conference on a possible Scandinavian software initiative called by Peter Naur in Copenhagen 1970. This was a position I was soon to regret. In 1974 my thinking had advanced sufficiently for me to take part in organising the first international command language conference in Lund/Frostavallen [1]. Like many other people, I started to learn and compare command languages and think about how they could be improved and standardised.

Even before the Frostavallen conference, a number of activities were going on. Command languages had grown to be a major headache at many computer installations and different groups — American, Dutch and British — started to work on:

— inventories of existing command languages and their functions
— proposals for future machine-independent command languages
— compilation from machine-independent command languages to existing command languages.

An early proposal for a machine-independent command language was SJCL, developed by Code, Inc. on order from the U.S. Department of Defense in 1970–71. It was a rich language, already containing most of the facilities needed in a general command language. Unfortunately, this project was discontinued without any implementation attempt.

The Frostavallen conference became a landmark. It brought together most of the groups and individuals working in the field and gave us an opportunity to meet and exchange ideas.

One outcome of the conference was the establishment of a working group on command languages, IFIP WG 2.7 (Chairmen F. Hertweck, and from 1981 D. Beech) with the intent of fostering research in command languages. The working group issues a bulletin [2] at three to four-month intervals, recommended for all who want to keep up with the field, and in 1979 organised another working conference in Berchtesgaden [3]. Recently it started work on a frame-of-reference paper [4] for submission to the standardisation bodies.

Another outcome of the Lund conference was a general agreement on some fundamental aspects of command language standardisation:

— it would be possible to define and implement a standard command language;
— a command language was needed as a separate language;
— no existing command language was proposed as a standard, this being in marked contrast to the situation in programming languages;
— a general command language ought to have the form of a high level language, including variables and conditional statements.

The question whether a separate command language was needed was one of the big issues of the conference. There was a considerable body of opinion that command languages were unnecessary, that it would be better to extend the programming languages to take care of the extra facilities needed. Command languages were not obviously necessary in the way we accept programming languages to be; indeed, many of us remembered a time when they did not even exist. Nevertheless, there was a consensus, essentially remaining to this day, that the separate command language is necessary and has to serve a number of disparate needs.

(1) It is needed to interface to the different programming languages.
(2) It is needed for user identification and accounting.
(3) It is needed to control the order in which programs within an application system are run.
(4) It is needed to invoke ready-made programs which may not be the user's own.

(We included 'It is needed to request operating system resources' high up on this list, but nowadays that can be done from programming languages as well.)

The range and disparity of features is thus considerably greater than in a programming language.

Point 3 was the crucial one, because the opposition argued that it was easier to construct the whole job as one program and control the flow by conventional programming language tools. Therefore, we had to consider the reasons why we do break big programs into parts. They include lack of core storage and the need to avoid excessive compilation times. Different program modules may be written by different people at different times, creating a need for running them in sequence. In the end, everybody agreed to accept command languages for the time being, and the work of defining common languages started in earnest.

4.2.2 The BCS Working Party

The first machine independent command language actually to be implemented and used seems to have been UNIQUE at University of Nottingham (I. A. Newman *et al.*, in [1]). It was intended to provide both simple and sophisticated users with a high level interface to the university's ICL 1906A with the alternative of having the UNIQUE statements compiled instead for a CD 7600 or an IBM 360/67. Emphasis was placed on a powerful default-setting mechanism, use of keywords rather than positional parameters and task-related high level commands. By 1974, the system was already running 4000 jobs a week, catering for 80% to 90% of all users at the centre.

Other British projects at this time were GCL at UKEA Culham Laboratories (Dakin) and ABLE at Bristol University (Parsons). A good overview of these early standardisation developments – and their continuation up to 1977 – is given by Mason in the IFIP/WG 2.7 Bulletin ([2], No. 1, p. 24).

Out of the early interest in Britain for machine independent command languages grew the British Computer Society (BCS) Working Party on command languages (Chairman I. A. Newman). It worked actively for a number of years, regularly updating a Journal of Development [5], and in 1980 published its finding in a book.

The classification of users, or rather levels of use, has several times been a topic for discussion in command language committees. The one proposed by the BCS seems very satisfactory:

(1) Application packages without explicit file handling.
(2) Application packages with explicit file handling.
(3) Program development and debugging for own use.
(4) Tailoring systems for other people's use.

(5) Developing system programs and interfaces for a user community, and tailoring for machine and system efficiency.

Another problem topic has been the treatment of compilation. The problem here is that compilers usually work in different stages. Nowadays, most compilers produce an intermediate code (relocatable code or object code) that is then mapped or linked into absolute code, which is then loaded and executed. Oldtime compilers went directly to absolute code, and this happens in some load-and-go compilers today, even to the point that the absolute code cannot be saved for later runs. These processes are difficult to describe in a portable manner.

The BCS Group settled the question by postulating that from the user's point of view the compilation is a language check and preparation for a run. The possibility (if it indeed exists) of saving intermediate code is a time-saving feature, an optimisation, to be separated conceptually from the rest of the process. Incidentally, there is a very interesting discussion of message levels during compilation, including a demand for a message level where not only source code errors, but also non-standard language features used, should be signalled.

A third interesting discussion concerns the default problem. Heavy use of defaulting – which everybody agrees is necessary – carries with it definite difficulties for portability since much information will not be explicit. Widening this discussion, the BCS Group proposed a general User Environment Tailor that will not only specify defaults but also modify syntax, specify logon-logoff, expand filenames, modify responses and so on.

4.2.3 The CCL Proposal

One of the first developments within the IFIP/WG 2.7 framework occurred when a group at Denmark's Technical University, Lyngby (C. Gram *et al.*) presented preliminary specifications for a Common Command Language CCL [6]. It was test implemented on the IBM 370/165 of NEUCC (North European Computing Centre).

A number of important concepts were united in CCL. It was a high level command language containing variables, simple expressions, assignment statements and conditional and iterative statements.

It included a block structure concept; you could create a block out of a sequence of statements by surrounding them with **BEGIN** ... **END** and putting a label before the **BEGIN**. Execution of a block produced a status variable (named by the block label) that could control the continued execution. (See CCL example below, where STEP2 is a status variable.) If the status variable signalled an error and was not sensed immediately after execution of the block, the surrounding block would be exited and return the status variable to its host block; this would continue upwards until either the status variable was taken care of or the run was aborted.

Another interesting idea was the copying of global variables into inner blocks where they could be changed freely; this would not affect the original variable unless specifically requested.

CCL advanced thinking about files considerably. A file (even if empty) was defined as a container of data. The name of a file was connected to a hierarchy of users. See figure below, where each ○ means a user and each X a file:

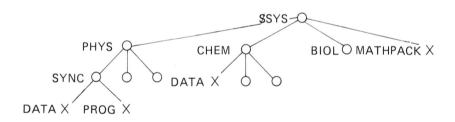

Example of user-file hierarchy in CCL.

The full name of the left-most user is $SYS.PHYS.SYNC. The full names of his files are $SYS.PHYS.SYNC.DATA and $SYS.PHYS.SYNC. PROG. But the user never has to use the full name for a file of his own. If he uses the name DATA, it will automatically be interpreted into a full name by adding a prefix. The first prefix to be tried will be the user's full name $SYS.PHYS.SYNC, and in this case DATA will be interpreted as $SYS.PHYS.SYNC.DATA. If he had used the name MATHPACK, this prefix would not work since there is no file

$SYS.PHYS.SYNC.MATHPACK. The interpreter would then successively try shorter chains, i.e. $SYS.PHYS and finally $SYS. Using $SYS would yield the name $SYS.MATHPACK (the rightmost file in the diagram) and this would be the interpretation of MATHPACK. In order to reach the file DATA under CHEM, the user would have to specify the name CHEM.DATA, which would be interpreted as $SYS.CHEM.DATA.

Files belonging to a user or his sub-users were accessible to him for reading and writing; those belonging to users at nodes encountered on the way to the system manager at the top of the hierarchy were accessible for reading only; other files were inaccessible, unless explicitly made public. Thus a system of automatic protection was created.

The creation and naming of files was done in a manner inspired by Simula. A file was created by a statement like

TRANS := FILE ON DISK;

The right hand expression is a 'file expression', and calling it creates a file on disk and a pointer to that file. The pointer is stored in the variable TRANS, through which we can now reach the file. Creating a second name for the same file now becomes very simple: TR := TRANS (the pointer is copied). The file now exists as long as there is any variable pointing to it, after which it is deleted ('garbage collection').

The problem of 'connecting' command language files to internal files within the program was settled once and for all by regarding it as a case of parameter passing. The program execution is, in effect, a procedure call with the command language file as the actual parameter, and the internal file as the formal parameter. Simple CCL commands like

EXTERNAL TRANS := FILE ON DISK;
RUN FILE := MY.ABS.PROG1, #1 := TRANS;

replaced various complex sequences like

```
@ASG,UP TRANS              //GO.SYSLMOD  DD  DSN=MY.ABS
@USE 1,TRANS        or                       (PROG1)
@XQT MY.PROG1              //FT01F001    DD  DSN=NN.TRANS,
                                             DISP=(NEW,PASS)
```

77

The language contained many facilites for file creation and handling, and for compiling, linking and executing programs with a minimum of commands. About the only important concept missing was the procedure concept. Some of CCL's facilities are hinted at in the example which follows (comments in right hand column):

```
CCLDEMO: JOB (FREE)                       (run's name and account)
BEGIN PROJECT := NN;
    EXTERNAL TRANS := FILE ON DISK;       (a disk file is created)
STEP1:RUN FILE := MY.ABS.PROG1,           (execution of an absolute
    #1 := TRANS,                           program; the program's file
    #5 := *;                               no. 1 and no. 5 are assigned,
— —                                        file 5 takes data, delimited
⟨data⟩                                     by − − + +, from the job
+ +                                        stream)
STEP2:BEGIN
    FORTRAN IN := MY.SOURCE.PROG2;        (compilation)
    RUN OBJLIB := MY.OBJLIB,              (linking with own library)
        #5 := TRANS,
        #0 := FILE ON TAPE('4711'),       (call for tapes no. 4711 and
        #1 := FILE ON TAPE('4712');        4712)
END STEP2;
IF STEP2 < WARNING THEN                    (if step 2 went right, delete
REMOVE TRANS;                              transaction file)
END JOB
```

Example of CCL.

CCL marked an important step by being the first such language to be implemented on machines and to be proposed — however modestly — as a possible standard. It had a profound influence on my own work, which resulted in a Univac 1100 implementation besides the IBM 360/165 one, with official support from the Swedish Board of Technical Development.

4.2.4 Networks and Command Languages – the Kiwinet Project

One of the really difficult questions connected with command languages has long been their relation to networks. Connecting computers of different manufacture into networks has been going on for some ten years. The primary purpose of a network is to make available to a wide range of users the databases or programs or special computing power present in the different component computers of the network. To be more precise, the purpose is to make these resources *easily* available; the user should be able to connect to different computers from the same terminal with a simple protocol. A typical exponent of this philosophy is the Arpanet. But without a common command language you still have to be aware of which computer you are using and use its command language and local programming language dialects. Some groups started to discuss the possibility of a common network command language; we may mention the Cyclades Network (France), the Ein Cost 11 (Switzerland), the NPL-NCC (United Kingdom) and Kiwinet (New Zealand). I shall go deeper into this last project because it has led to a complete and fairly well documented command language proposal.

The Kiwinet project was started as a university project in 1975, but the interested parties now include other computer centres with a wide range of computers. The project committee contacted C. Unger of the Dortmund University Group and H. Sayani, then chairman of the ANSI/X3H1 command language subcommittee, and also investigated the best manufacturer-supplied command languages, the Burroughs WFL and ICL SCL, as candidates. Eventually, it was decided to build a new command language starting from some of the SCL concepts [7, 8].

A network command language can have at least four different purposes, as D. Rayner once pointed out ([2], No. 1, p. 17):

(1) to provide a network standard command language;

(2) to provide uniform access to files as if the network had a single filing system;

(3) to provide an interface for users who want to view the network as a single computer facility;

(4) to enable users to run different parts of the same job on different computers and pass data between them, possibly with some degree of synchronised parallelism.

Kiwinet intends to provide (1) and (4) but not (2) and (3), that is, the user has to be well aware that there are different nodes in the network and he can route his job and data between these, using an AT clause and a SITE attribute.

The Kiwinet project defines three languages, a command language NCL, a response language NRL, and a network access language NAL (the latter need not concern us here, however).

The NCL is interesting not only because it covers the network aspect, but also because it is a very comprehensive language. It recognises variables of the modes integer, real, boolean and string (data types are called 'modes' in this system). Most of these modes can be compounded into arrays, sets or queues. Further, it recognises events, files, peripherals and environments. The treatment of these concepts seems definitive; the list of peripheral attributes has 24 entries, file attributes 46 entries, and environment attributes 20 entries. The file attributes cover the logical and physical blocking of the file, its history, owner, access rights, use mode, labelling, etc. This does not mean that every user will have to deal with these properties of all his files; but they will be available if and when needed.

The NCL is complemented with many system macros to handle files and environments, compile and execute, logon-logoff and so on. The definition of a macro or code procedure allows for use of both keywords and defaults (signalled in the declaration by ( ) and :=, respectively). Imagine the following declaration has been made:

```
MACRO WHATSIT = (INTEGER (COPIES)    C
                ,REF FILE (INPUT)     INF   := FILEA
                ,REF FILE (OUTPUT)    OUTP  := FILEB
                ,STRING (TEXT)        T
                ,REF INT              R     := X);
```

Here are some examples of calls using positional parameters, keyword parameters or a mix of both. The meaning is explained in terms of the complete positional parameter call.

```
Call:       WHATSIT(5,MYFILE,,"STOP",X);
Meaning:    WHATSIT(5,MYFILE,FILEB,"STOP",X);

Call:       WHATSIT(INPUT:="GO",COPIES=3);
Meaning:    WHATSIT(3,MYFILE,FILEB,"GO",X);
```

Call: WHATSIT(5,TEXT:="STOP",INT1);
Meaning: WHATSIT(5,FILEA,FILEB,"STOP",INT1);

A new, ground-breaking attempt in this project is the definition of a response language with the purpose of giving at least a minimum range of error types to be explicitly handled and a minimum requirement for error message formats.

4.2.5 The Nicola Project

In close contact with the Kiwinet people, another group (C. Unger *et al.*) in Dortmund studied and elaborated the concept of abstract machines. The start of serious research into this topic was a very welcome development. Many problems all over the language field are basically problems of faulty or inconsistent abstraction.

The group notes that most users do not need a very detailed knowledge of the computer system. A user is better served by an abstract model of the system, an 'abstract machine' (AM). This machine abstracts from the 'real' machine and therefore hides some details in order to offer a simple application-oriented interface to the user. There will be various levels of these AMs according to different kinds of users (scientific, administrative, etc.). We need therefore to define a basic abstract machine (BAM) from which all other AMs may be derived, step by step.

An AM is a collection of the following items:

(1) a user oriented description of the syntax and semantics of the command language and the response language;
(2) a set of modes available to the user;
(3) a default environment of the user.

The mechanism for definition of a new AM from an existing one must be included in the command language. One of the things necessary is to define the response handling. Responses in the lower (= less abstract) AM may no longer be meaningful at a higher level of abstraction. Therefore the UE ('undesired event') giving rise to the response will have to be reformulated so that it is meaningful to the new user. All this will have to be done explicitly when defining the new AM.

It will be most interesting to see the effect of the implementation of these ideas by the Kiwinet and Nicola groups and to see them in use. The Nicola-Kiwinet report [9] was recently accepted as a frame-of-reference paper by ANS X3H1.

4.2.6 The Unix System

Let us now turn to another interesting command language, this time in the United States, namely the Unix system at Bell Laboratories.

The Unix system seems to be one of those things that just happened. In the words of the reference [10]: 'Although the basic UNIX system was literally developed in an attic by two people in a year, and has been available only as an unsupported package, the benefits it provides are so compelling that currently there are nearly 1000 UNIX systems scattered around the world'. That makes it easily the most successful so far of all machine-independent command languages (or so I thought until hearing about the even more wide-spread CP/M, much in vogue for microcomputers).

The file system of Unix has a fairly conventional hierarchic structure, but it has a couple of important new user concepts too:

(1) Directories are files. That means the handling of a directory, for example, listing it or searching it, is done by ordinary user programs;

(2) A file is just a sequence of bytes. This is so revolutionary that it is best to point out the attributes a Unix file does not have:
 — there are no tracks or cylinders or other physical device characteristics;
 — there are no physical or logical records or associated counts — the only bytes are the ones put there by the user;
 — no fixed/variable length distinction, no visible blocking or buffering;
 — no pre-allocation of file space — the file is always exactly as big as you made it;
 — no access methods — the bytes are accessible in any order, and all files are identical in form.

Peripherals are also files in this system, organised in a special directory for convenience. This means, for example, that the same program (written in the C programming language) that can be used to copy files also becomes a spooling program.

When a user logs into the Unix system, a command interpreter called the Shell accepts commands from the terminal and interprets them as requests to run programs. Any program file that is executed in Unix has two files opened for it automatically, an input and an output file that are connected to the user's active terminal. These may be redirected before execution:

    program <in >out

instructs the Shell to arrange that 'program' take its input from 'in' and place its output on 'out'; 'program' itself is unaware of the change.

It is part of the Unix philosophy to run simple programs in sequence to produce interesting results. As an example, suppose we have to find out how many times user 'joe' is at present logged in. It can be done by running three programs:

who >userlist	'who' produces a list of everybody logged in on 'userlist'.
grep joe <userlist >joelist	'grep' searches 'userlist' for occurrences of the pattern 'joe' and stores them in 'joelist'.
wc <joelist	'wc' counts the length of 'joelist' = the number of logins requested!

This seems compact enough, but can be written in one line as follows:

who | grep joe | wc

The vertical line | has the effect that the output of its left-hand side is used as input to its right-hand side. This technique, called 'pipe-lining' for easily understandable reasons, does away with the intermediate files 'userlist' and 'joelist'. But not only that. It sweeps away the concept of the job-step, which was really only a hold-over from primitive command languages, and in effect introduces the file manipulation expression.

4.2.7 APL as a Command Language

I should like to mention APL too, since it is really a fusion of command language and programming language. The ability of the APL user to switch between definition mode and execution mode gives a better description of the compile-execute process than any command language proposed so far:

∇ P	switch to definition mode to define procedure P
⟨program⟩	enter program, including read statements
∇	switch back to execution mode
P	execute P
⟨data⟩	enter data as requested by read statements in P

83

4.2.8 The Appearance of File Handling in Fortran

The acceptance of the Fortran 77 standard had a bearing on the relation between programming languages and command languages which was hardly noticed at the time. I am referring to the appearance of file handling commands within Fortran.

Up to then we had more or less taken it for granted that file handling belonged to the realm of command languages. Part of the reason for this was that some operating systems did not allow files to be attached to a run other than at command language level. With the evolution of operating systems, this restriction is gradually being eased, but there are still implementations of Fortran 77 that allow the user to attach files with OPEN, but require him to attach the file at command language level too, which makes the OPEN statement redundant. Such an implementation, while perhaps standard conforming in letter, is against the spirit of the OPEN statement, i.e. that it should be a tool for dynamic file handling.

But dynamic file handling carries with it a certain risk. Two active batch runs may each call for exclusive use of a file that the other one is already using. This crossing of requests (sometimes called 'deadly embrace') makes both runs wait for each other indefinitely until the operator intervenes. This risk will be eliminated if exclusive use of files is restricted and always confined to command language level, so the system can check that the file is available before the run is started.

4.2.9 The CODASYL COSCL Proposal

In May 1979, CODASYL's command language group published specifications for a general command language COSCL [11]. This is a major event, because of the great influence wielded by CODASYL, even though the responsibility for standardisation falls not on CODASYL, but rather on ANSI X3H1 which recently published design specifications for a standard command language (see below). But CODASYL's previous efforts in the ADP field, Cobol and DBML, have had such profound influence on ADP that one rather expects COSCL to be accepted too.

COSCL was the first proposal to present explicitly the whole range of facilities needed in a command language. It contains 40-odd commands which can be grouped into logon/logoff, defaults and synonyms, file and device handling, compilation/linkage/execution of programs, utilities, handling of parallel sessions, debugging, and drop-through to host language. These will be discussed under their respective headings later. It has variables, modern control structures, and a procedure concept. The syntax is Cobol-style, somewhat wordy for interactive use and not as elegant as, for example, that of CCL. There are some interesting ideas for the handling of procedure parameters; both their number and types may vary and can be retrieved from within the procedure.

Here is the same example in COSCL, as previously given for CCL. It corresponds line by line to the CCL example, except for the BEGIN and END of STEP2. Note the use of the ON-END_ON clause for exception handling. The ... means that the statement continues on the next line.

```
LOGON USER = FREE, SESSION = COSCLDEMO
DEFAULT HOME DIRECTORY = NN
CATALOG TRANS, TEMPORARY, DISK
STEP1: MY.ABS.PROG1 . . .
        #1 = TRANS, . . .
        #5 = D
BEGIN_DATA D
⟨data⟩
END_DATA
STEP2 = 0; ON PROGRAM_FAULT STEP2 = 1 END_ON
ALLOCATE INTAPE TO TAPE_4711; ALLOCATE OUTTAPE TO
        TAPE_4712
    FORTRAN INPUT = MY.SOURCE.PROG2 OBJECT = OB
    LINK MODULE = OB, LIBRARY = MY.OBJLIB, PROGRAM = P
    P  #5 = TRANS, . . .
        #0 = INTAPE, . . .
        #1 = OUTTAPE
    IF STEP2 < 1 THEN . . .
        DELETE TRANS
LOGOFF
```

Example of COSCL.

4.2.10 Official Standardisation Work within ANSI and ISO

All the committees and groups mentioned so far have been bodies concerned with fostering research and development and making proposals for command languages, but they are not bodies officially charged with setting standards. Now we shall see what the standards bodies did about the command language problem. As usual, the most important bodies in this connection are the American National Standards Institute (ANSI) and the International Standards Organisation (ISO).

ANSI made a SPARC (Standards Planning and Requirements Committee) study as early as 1969 and established a subcommittee X3H1 on command languages in the middle 1970s. Under the chairmanship of Lois C. Frampton, it worked out a set of Functional Requirements and Design Criteria [12]. The goal was to define an OSCRL (Operating System Command and Response Language) to cover a very broad range of environments and users, and yet implementable on today's systems without unduly degrading performance. Special stress was laid on a clean and consistent syntax and facilities that would help and protect the casual user.

At first it seemed that ANSI X3H1 would use these requirements and criteria as tools to compare and evaluate proposals that would be submitted from outside the committee. When the Nicola and Codasyl papers were submitted, they were accepted as frame-of-reference papers. By this time, however, the committee had started work on a full language proposal of its own, now under the chairmanship of Vance Miller. At the time of writing, it is too early to say something about the flavour of this proposal. Public review is expected early in 1984.

While this went on, ISO had been marking time, no member body having taken steps to introduce command languages as a working item until a proposal from France was laid before the ISO TC97 SC5 (programming language subcommittee) at its October 1981 meeting in Old Windsor. It was decided to hold an ad hoc meeting in Dublin April 1982 with Ireland as convenor. At this meeting it was decided to establish liaison with ISO TC97 SC16 (Open Systems Interconnection) to avoid duplication of work. A formal proposal for command language as a work item was recently approved by letter ballot.

I should like to summarise the results of international research as consisting of the following ideas:

— a general command language is needed;
— it should be a new language, none of the existing manufacturers' languages will do;

— it should be high level, including variables and conditional statements;
— it should call programs in other languages as subprograms, passing and receiving parameters;
— it should have a file system, preferably of the Unix type, but in any case one that is compatible between different programming languages;
— it should have a hierarchical system for naming its entities; such a naming system would automatically confer a certain level of protection.

We have now had an overview of the history of command language standardisation. This gives us a framework, but still not a complete one. Before we are ready to outline solutions to the problems mentioned at the start of this chapter we have to introduce some basic ideas.

4.3 SOME BASIC CONCEPTS

4.3.1 The Principle of Algorithmic Information
To begin with, I should like to remind you of the distinction discussed back in Chapter 1 between algorithmic, optimising, and environmental information. This principle has wide application in command languages.

You will remember that we formulated the following general rules:

(1) The algorithmic information should be 100% portable.
(2) The optimising information may vary from system to system. One should try to leave as much of the optimising to the system as possible. When this is not possible, the information should be in as machine-independent a form as possible. At least it should follow some standard rules of syntax.
(3) For environmental information, portability is often not possible or even of interest. If a person B takes over an application from a person A at another computing center, customer information and tape numbers *should* be changed. In these cases the standard needs to go no farther than general rules for how these things should be expressed in the command language.

Now to some concrete applications of these concepts in command languages.

Typical optimising information is the *choice of medium* to store a file. The result of a run, or series of runs, is independent of whether intermediate storage was on tape, disk or drum. The choice of medium is optimising information, we try to minimise the combined cost of storing the data and processing them. This information should be as portable as possible. For example, it is better to define a file's size and access method and let the system choose the medium, than to direct the file unconditionally to disk or drum.

A similar piece of optimising information is the *block size*; by controlling it we try to find the right balance between core storage and I/O time.

Under this heading we also classify the compression of files in order to take away obsolete elements. On one system the user may have to think actively about compressing files, while another does it automatically.

So far, the applications have been fairly easy to agree on. But the next one is controversial. It is the handling of compile-link-go, and it is so important that I shall return to it later and give it a heading of its own.

4.3.2 Normal Form

Another basic concept mentioned earlier that we need to have as a background to our thinking is the concept of a 'normal form' for application processes.

We shall define a *process* as a sequence of one or more program executions, which accept input from disk storage files or external devices and produce results on files and/or external devices. For such a process to be portable, certain conditions must be fulfilled.

One is that the programs to be executed in the process are in source from, i.e. not in some computer's internal code. Another is that the programs must be complete in the sense that any library subroutines called by them must be explicitly known in source form; we cannot be satisfied with a reference to a name in the library, which may be a local resource which varies over time. Furthermore, the input and output files should be character files, as opposed to binary files which would be machine dependent. We need not exclude the possibility that certain programs within the process produce binary files as intermediate results (e.g. the unformatted files of standard Fortran) but if so these must be read back by programs later in the process. Similarly, an object program may be used only by being linked and then executed; it may not, for example, be listed.

A process fulfilling these conditions is said to be in *normal form*.

Essentially, it means that the job is completely defined as it stands.

Examples of entities not in normal form are programs in object form, catalogued files referenced by name only, and generally constructs that are understandable only if you know the previous history of the program system and its operative defaults. The non-normal form will often be much shorter than normal form, that being the reason for using it. From the porting point of view, only the normal form need be considered. Environmental information may appear in the normal form, but as mentioned above that is the information we want to change when porting.

4.3.3 Separation of Processing from I/O

A valuable method for simplifying command language problems is to separate processing, in the sense defined below, from input/output.

If one is going to draw a picture on the plotter, for example, this should take place via an intermediary file which describes the picture by a string of characters. In this way one can separate a graphic process into two parts: first, the generation part, which only depends on the application and is a portable Fortran program, and second, the drawing part, which is only dependent on the physical unit one draws on and the actual computer system. Apart from the gain in portability, there is the essential practical advantage that one can easily choose which graphical unit one wants to output the picture to; for example, one can send it to a video unit if one is testing a program, to a plotter if one runs regularly, and to a reserve plotter if the plotter is out of order.

Similar solutions can be used for input and output of punched cards, paper tape and of the many different kinds of magnetic tapes which one may have to handle in a computing center. With magnetic tapes, problems may turn up if the data sets are so large that the tape file cannot be stored as a disk file. But one should then in any case convert external tapes to and from the site's standard magnetic tapes instead of inputting all kinds of tapes directly into the application programs.

Another important practical advantage is that you often can write a command language sequence once and for all for such separate I/O. It is no mean advantage — these special command language sequences are often an order of magnitude more complicated than those for ordinary program executions.

4.3.4 Implementation Considerations

What can the user do in the way of implementing a common command language or, barring that, to facilitate porting of command language sequences? Evidently that is going to depend a lot on the operating system. The answer will be very different from system to system, depending on such circumstances as:

— does the operating system allow dynamic file handling?
     otherwise you will probably be restricted to a pre-processor for batch;
— is there a command language procedure facility?
     that will be a great help.

In any case, a very first step is always possible. That is to set down a translation procedure in writing. This will force you to think through your existing command language in terms of the commands the user would like to have; it will give you a manual of tested and recommended sequences to give to your users. You can implement many commands just by writing command language procedures or programming language programs, or interfacing to existing ones.

4.3.5 Command Languages versus Programming Languages

We have seen above that as time has passed, it has become natural to wish for programming language facilities (variables, conditional statements, etc.) in command languages. We have further seen that classical command language features like file handling turn up in programming languages. Finally we have seen a command language, Unix, become so easy to use that it becomes a convenient tool for non-professional users, in stark contrast to the classical command languages which are rather felt as a hindrance to work.

As a natural conclusion of this development we shall from now on assume that the same syntax and features are useful in both control and programming languages, unless otherwise proved. We are not abolishing the command language, but recognising it as a level above the programming language. And, as we have already pointed out, an execution means that the command language calls a main program written in a programming language, transmitting files and other data as parameters.

4.4 COMMAND LANGUAGE ISSUES

We shall now go through the command language issues one by one, drawing freely on COSCL and alternative proposals and evaluating them according to the principles outlined above. I shall try to take them more or less in order of importance, starting with the ones I use every day. There is a lot of ground to cover, so be prepared for a bit of slogging.

4.4.1 Logon/Logoff

LOGON and LOGOFF are among the commands that every command language proposal include. They are the commands that initiate and terminate a user's session, i.e. a period of interaction with the system. The COSCL LOGON has parameters for user code and password, project name, session name, and a way of specifying local information like resource limits, priority, etc., which we have already classified as environmental information with limited need for portability. The COSCL commands in question include the useful possibility of having a user-defined set of commands executed automatically immediately after logon and immediately before logoff, and to save an environment at logoff and restore it at logon.

A separate command USING is employed to set limits to the physical resources that will be used in the session.

The first point to note is that LOGON has a special standing in that it is given in another environment than that of all other commands of a command language. The other commands presume that the system is in command language mode; LOGON is given to the system in the pre-logon mode when your terminal has just been connected. In this situation there is precious little you can do except logon. Our local system will indeed accept any input at this point as a token of interest and prompt you for user identification and password. I really like this better than an explicit LOGON command, but let us not make an issue out of it.

As for user identification, there is another point to make. The fact that we give user identification in a computer language may be a temporary condition depending on technology. Twenty years ago, the user was identified by his looks when he entered the machine room: another twenty years from now he may identify himself by a plastic card. Something like it happened in telephony where a line first was set up by two researchers throwing switches, then by oral instruction to a telephone operator, until the dial was finally introduced.

4.4.2 Syntax for Calling Programs and Procedures

Calling a program or procedure is the minimum useful thing one could do after a logon. The syntax for it is more or less similar in all languages except for the very elegant pipelining facility in Unix and the facility for showing the intent or direction of parameters. I have not made up my mind about proposing the Unix syntax, because it seems to be specifically a command language syntax, and I would prefer to have roughly the same syntax in all languages (we shall discuss this in the next chapter). That leaves us with the standard call, consisting of the procedure name followed by keyword parameters, but enhanced with $<$ and $>$ for in and out parameters, respectively:

  MY_PROG IN$<$FILE1, OUT$>$FILE2

The program called might be a language processor, e.g. APL, Basic or Ada, and for a user of one of those languages, which have their own mechanism for program calls and file handling, the logon and the language call will be all the user ever sees of the common command language.

4.4.3 Compile-Link-Go

For us lesser mortals, the time has now come to study the compile-link-go process used in so many command languages.

  There are two views on this complex of problems. According to one, compilation is a process like any other; it produces an object element which the user is conscious of and links to an executable program by a LINK command. This is the way that, for example, COSCL handles the matter. According to the other view, compilation and linkage is something which should take place behind the scenes without the user being conscious of it. This is the view of APL, for example, which in itself combines programming language and command language. The latter is evidently more convenient for the user, and experiments done within my research project show that it is possible to do it without loss of efficiency. We give an example opposite comparing the COSCL and APL syntax for a simple compile and run. (A library LIB is supposed to exist, and is extended with SUB before compiling and running the main program.)

  The COSCL sequence accomplishes the same thing as the APL sequence in the algorithmic sense — it adds a subroutine to the library LIB and then compiles, links and executes the main program. In addition, it has a lot of optimising capability that the APL sequence lacks. The intermediate forms, the object modules of SUB and MAIN, are accessible, and you may in any run use those modules whose source code is unchanged from the previous run for linkage and execution, thus saving compiling time. By contrast, the APL procedures seem to exist only in source form, and for all we know they are recompiled or even interpreted in each run.

```
FORTRAN INPUT=SUB, OBJECT=LIB.SUB          ) LOAD LIB
BEGIN_DATA FILE=SUB                        ∇ SUB
⟨subroutine SUB⟩                           ⟨subroutine SUB⟩
END_DATA                                   ∇
FORTRAN MAIN, OBJMAIN
BEGIN_DATA MAIN                            ∇ P
⟨main program⟩                            ⟨main program⟩
END_DATA                                   ∇
LINK MODULE=OBJMAIN, LIBRARY=LIB, . . .
    PROGRAM=P
P                                          P
```

Sample compile-link-go in COSCL and APL.

I am in no doubt about preferring the APL method. It is concise and easy for an amateur user to understand and remember. On many systems it can be implemented efficiently by compiling each procedure the first time it is called and saving the object module. On subsequent calls the object module would be recompiled only if the source code had been changed since the previous call. If this implementation were not efficient enough, means could be devised to supply the optimising information separately from the algorithmic; for example, commands like SAVE SUB and DO_NOT_SAVE P, or even TEST P, might be used to override the normal routine.

We must note that even in the simple APL scheme two pieces of information are needed besides the program: the language it is written in, and the library that supplements it in case it is not self-supporting. In the APL environment, the language is by implication APL (we achieved this by calling the APL processor). We should like to have a similar mechanism for setting up Fortran, for example, as the default language for a session, and perhaps an option LANG=FORTRAN on the program call to allow a temporary language switch. The library specification should be contained in the program, and the USING statement in Fortran 8X is the answer to this need.

While we wait for these facilities, there is a practical step we can take, and that is to make a habit of storing each program unit surrounded by the commands necessary to compile and link it, instead of keeping these as a special command language sequence. That will save you time and trouble when you come back to old projects.

93

4.4.4 Overlaying Large Programs

Before leaving the compile-link complex, let us also consider the overlaying of large programs.

The problem is classic. The program, including its data areas, is too large to fit into the available core storage, at least if you write it in a straightforward way. You are faced with trying to shrink it to manageable proportions. On many systems it is possible to do this by allowing subroutines, that never have to be active simultaneously, to share the same storage. Quite often you will be able to split even the bulk of the main program into subroutines that will be executed in sequence. Doing the splitting and planning the overlays calls for some knowledge of the program, in particular of the interplay between subroutines and the frequency with which they are called.

How the intended storage sharing is described to the system is another matter. In an Algol program it is quite natural to do it with simple keywords within the program, but Fortran, featuring separate compilation, has usually treated it in another way. The layout is normally described during the linkage phase, and consists of associating with each other those subroutines that are to share storage. The description of this association could be done machine-independently; a very simple solution could be an OVERLAY command, placed in the main program just as the USING command, e.g.

    OVERLAY A, B, C
    OVERLAY TEMP, STRESS, DISPL

If the language feature specifying overlays can be machine-independent, the actual need for overlay is of course very machine-dependent. Not only does the available storage vary from system to system, but these days many systems allow so-called virtual storage, i.e. but programmer can write programs as if the storage were unlimited, and the system handles the overlaying dynamically.

Interestingly, no current machine-independent command proposal includes an overlay facility. The committees may feel that the problem is on its way out because of larger machines and virtual storage, or the command language committees may consider it to be a problem for programming languages committees and vice versa.

4.4.5 File Handling

No user above the complete amateur can avoid file handling. As we have seen, Fortran 77 already allows several file operations, including the facility to find out whether a file is available and then attach it to the program. It would be nice to coordinate this process, so that the same facilities become available in command language and in different programming languages. Such a file handling standard should include:

— facilities for creating, deleting and handling of files
— a system for hierarchical naming of files
— library files (this could be a special case of hierarchical naming, or they could be groups of files listed in directories that are themselves files)
— protection against undesired access (this could also be an extension of the naming scheme with passwords and keys)
— ways of controlling the placing of files on media and reservation of space for them
— ways of removing rarely used files to background storage
— handling of generations of files.

COSCL proposes the following commands for file handling:

```
CATALOG FILE=name, LIFE=perm,
    CYCLE=cycle, MAX_CYCLES=maxc,
    VERSION=ver, TYPE=type, LANGUAGE=lang,
    RIGHTS=(OWNER= . . ., SYSTEM= . . ., GROUP= . . ., WORLD= . . .),
    SHARING=pop, READ=rkey, WRITE=wkey, RUN=xkey,
    DEVICE=dev, VOLUME=vol, MAX_SIZE=maxs, LIKE=name_2
```

perm=*TEMPORARY*!PERMANENT!CONDITIONAL specifies the life-time of
                    the file;
cycle, maxc: the cycle number and maximum number of cycles;
ver, type, lang: establish file attributes;
RIGHTS and pop: establish rights for various groups of users;
rkey, wkey, xkey: provide different types of access;
dev, vol, maxs: control the storage of the file;
LIKE: allows you to copy unspecified attributes from name_2.

CHANGE	(same parameters as CATALOG, except for dev and vol)
DELETE	FILE=name, VARIABLE=var, SYNONYM=id
ATTACH	FILE=name, SYNONYM=synonym, ACCESS=sha, READ=rkey, WRITE=wkey, RUN=xkey
FREE	FILE=name

and finally two commands especially for library files: DISPLAY and CONTRACT.

The Fortran 77 commands have been described earlier, but we shall repeat them briefly here for convenience. Some of the parameters have been renamed to avoid confusion with COSCL terms.

OPEN   (unit, iostatus, err-label, file, permanence, dirseq, fm, rl)

INQUIRE (unit|file, iostatus, err-label, exist, opened, file|unit, dirseq, fm, rl, nextrec)

CLOSE   (unit, iostat, err-label, permanence)

If we compare these two proposals, some interesting differences and similarities come to light.

If we begin with the main commands and the control of the file's permanence, or life-time, the two proposals match fairly well. COSCL tallies directly with the elementary facilities necessary: the creation, changing, and deletion of the file, the attaching of it to a run and the subsequent detaching, and finally the special operation of contraction. These elementary operations can be mapped to Fortran in the following ways:

CATALOG: OPEN with STATUS=NEW or SCRATCH, followed by
          CLOSE with STATUS=KEEP
CHANGE: OPEN with STATUS=OLD and new parameter values
DELETE: CLOSE with STATUS=DELETE
ATTACH: OPEN
FREE: CLOSE

Here the similarity ends. All parameters except file-name and permanence are different. While this contradicts our presumption that languages do not have to be different unless it is proved, it is interesting to note that the similarity is mainly in the algorithmic information — the actions that create and delete a file and thus have a bearing on the result. The differences appear in the environmental and optimising information. We shall go through the COSCL parameters in detail, throwing a glance now and then at Fortran and, of course, at the very simple file concept of Unix.

We shall begin with the cycle attribute and max-cycles, (which are still algorithmic information). The COSCL philosophy is that every new write to a file creates a new cycle of it. This is very convenient, and what storage problems may appear should be controlled by rapid deletion of old cycles. Max-cycles is interesting and useful. It seems to me that it makes CONTRACT superfluous: the system can contract your file automatically and remove old cycles when it needs the space. As for the generation parameter. I should like to see it syntactically as part of the file name, e.g. MY_FILE(17) would be cycle 17 and MY_FILE(−2) the 'grandfather' of the current cycle.

Next we come to parameters that control the type of file: the type, version and language attributes. (Fortran's FORMATTED parameter comes under this heading too.) The type attribute can specify a file as all sorts of things: data, library, source, object, executable, printfile, text, workspace, etc. The version attribute seems to do much the same thing. These parameters I would rather be without: if the system needs to know what type of information there is in a file in order to handle it, it will have to take note when I start writing.

We then come to the parameters that control the allocation of the file to physical storage: device, volume and max-size, and Fortran's ACCESS=DIRECT or SEQUENTIAL. This is optimising information, and thus should be given in as machine-independent a form as possible if portability is a concern. The max-size and dirseq parameters should be used normally when you are happy to let the system do the physical allocation of the file. (COSCL probably intended max-size to be used to set a limit to how large the file could be. I regard the setting of max-size to be largely unnecessary information and would rather let the system use it as a guide to choose between large, slow devices and small, fast devices.)

In contrast, device and volume should be used when you have to control the allocation in detail, say because you must have a special tape drive and reel. In this case you actually need a couple of extra parameters:

BLKSIZE=bs   where bs is the block size,
LABEL=lab   to control labelling, and
REMOVABLE=yesno

Note the alternative, discussed under separation of I/O, of letting the transfer to specific external media always be a separate spooling operation.

The figure below shows more and less portable ways of giving the same information. (SIZEs are given in k bytes.)

DEVICE=TAPE   ACCESS=SERIAL, SIZE=1000

DEVICE=DISK_123   ACCESS=RANDOM, SIZE=50,
                           REMOVABLE=YES

More or less portable storage allocation.

The right-hand expressions, while longer, are evidently much less restrictive than the left-hand ones. The DEVICE=TAPE, taken literally, would disqualify a tape-less machine for the job, whereas the corresponding right-hand command makes it clear that we can simulate the tape on a large disk. In the second case, having only the information to the left, we would have to give up if the installation did not allow private disks; the right-hand side shows that it is not the size of the disk but rather the ability to remove it that is important, and therefore we may simulate the private disk on drum during processing and spool it to tape for storage between jobs.

4.4.6 Protection

Finally we come to the question of access rights (the rights, access-keys and sharing parameters). COSCL proposes that there be seven types of access rights: READ, WRITE, EXECUTE, APPEND, EXCLUSIVE, CHANGE and DELETE. The session that catalogues the file (or changes it) can extend different rights to SYSTEM, OWNER, PROJECT, WORLD or a USER-LIST, or to users who know the key for an access right. Again it seems to me that this is valid and useful, and a clear improvement over earlier schemes that only differentiated between READ and WRITE. I have a minor quibble about EXCLUSIVE which seems to me to belong only to the ATTACH, not the to CATALOG command. (I do not like it there either, on account of the risk for deadly embrace mentioned earlier — and if each write creates a new cycle, why do we need it at all? — but at least that is where it does the least harm.) Another minor point is that WRITE and CHANGE seem to me to be the same thing, so it boils down to five: READ, WRITE, EXECUTE, APPEND, and DELETE. Of these, WRITE is obviously the most powerful and must reasonably include all the others; it is rather easy to think up concrete applications for each of these other access rights alone:

READ	for a data file accessible to colleagues
EXECUTE	for a program that may be used but not copied
APPEND	for the master log file, which is a kind of mail box
DELETE	for the system manager who may delete a disused file

Normally, I am quite satisfied with the implicit protection given by a hierarchical file structure like that of CCL where the main protection is the simple one that you have to know a file's name and project identification to access it. CCL implicitly allows WRITE access to the file's owner, and READ access to sub-projects and neighbours.

I am no expert on the subject, but I believe this question of access rights, passwords, etc. has been somewhat overdone in the general discussion about command languages. Privacy, security and protection are currently in fashion and a lot of work goes into protection schemes. It is not that easy to pilfer other people's data, even when the protection level is fairly low. You have to know a file name, probably an account name too; you have to identify yourself to the system, so any access may be checked later on; and you have to be able to get useful information out of the file. Most people I know have too much trouble getting useful information out of their own files to bother with other people's files. I am not saying computer crime doesn't occur and cannot be very serious – I just doubt whether it can be prevented by password schemes. And I get downright uneasy about proposals that start out by saying that the whole command language must be designed around the need for security. To draw a parallel with building: that is the proper frame of mind if you are designing a bank vault or a bunker. It is hardly appropriate for an office building.

4.4.7 Routing of I/O

Routing of I/O is something that is needed for everyday work at a terminal. COSCL proposes the following commands:

DIVERT FROM=sce, TO=dest

sce is the file that is to be diverted to dest.

A normal use of DIVERT is to divert output from the default output file $OUTPUT to a user-defined file. This is done in order to be able to inspect the result on the screen before physically printing it. (You will recall that this facility is present even in Unix, though in a much more compact form.) Other files that are predefined and can be diverted are the input files $COMMAND and $INPUT and the output files $RESPONSE (for system responses) and $MONITOR (for logging all work on the terminal).

REVERT FILE=dest

undoes the effect of a previous DIVERT.

MONITOR MODE=onoff

enables or disables logging of terminal work.

ROUTE FILE=filename, DESTINATION=dev

This is a DIVERT to a physical device instead of to a logical file. To my mind, this is an interesting (but still unpolished) alternative to the DEVICE/VOLUME parameters of the CATALOG command, quite in keeping with the idea of separating I/O from processing. It will need some more parameters to do the job properly.

4.4.8 Libraries

It is very convenient to group program files into libraries (directories, in COSCL terminology). Libraries are used to provide the environment for single main programs: you can direct the system to pick all referenced but undefined subprograms from a library.

It is natural to use hierarchical naming for members of a library: We can imagine the library P made up of P.INPUT, P.PROC, P.OUTPUT, P.CHECK, etc. Most proposals think of a library as having a table of contents, which is itself a file, say P.$TOC, which is updated by the system and accessible to the user for reading, so he can easily search the library. Once a library has been defined, it can be copied and handled as a whole in different ways.

4.4.9 Background Storage

COSCL bypasses the question of a standardised handling of background storage. Some proposal is in order; background storage is an everyday concern and must be handled properly.

Background storage could be controlled by operations like:

```
ARCHIVE(FILE=fin)
RESTORE(FILE=fin)
PURGE(FILE=fin)
```

with obvious meanings. A specifier could be added to CATALOG:LIFE=li, where li is the number of days the file will be kept before being automatically archived.

4.4.10 Handling of Parallel Sessions

At first glance you might think the commands listed below are advanced facilities, but the first three at least are actually everyday tools for starting a batch session from an interactive session. The last three are maybe slightly more fancy, but useful. The facilities proposed in COSCL are:

SUBMIT	Start a parallel session
STATUS	Inquire about the status of a submitted session
CANCEL	Terminate a submitted session
OPERATOR	Communicate with operator
SEND	Send a message to a parallel session
RECEIVE	Receive a message from a parallel session

COSCL leaves the setting of priorities to the host language, perhaps wisely since priorities are often controlled not by priority degrees alone, but also by size of job, type of user, etc. There is nowhere a facility for controlling the specific resource MAX_TIME, which is a bit surprising since this device for aborting a program in an infinite loop has been with us since the beginning of command languages. It is crude, but nobody seems to have come up with anything better.

4.4.11 Exception Handling
COSCL provides a comprehensive repertoire of exception handling.

ON CONDITION=cond . . . END_ON

The ON . . . END_ON brackets allow the user to define action to be taken on the occurrence of an exception. The action can include a GO TO within the block being executed; alternatively, the RESUME command restarts execution before or after the interrupt. If an exception occurs within a block and is not handled by the user, a default action is taken. A SIGNAL statement can be used to fake an exception. I have no experience of this kind of scheme which originates from PL/I, and believe it is unnecessarily complicated. My preference is the CCL solution described earlier; I could certainly live with the COSCL proposal if it works.

4.4.12 Simple Variables and Control Constructs
I have said little about these so far. Though everybody agrees this should be in a new common command language, almost all of us have had to learn to live without them. There is a moral in this; if they had been absolutely necessary they would have been implemented in manufacturers' languages. But of course they will be wonderful to have once they appear. They will give the user quite new possibilities to make the processing depend on the existence or otherwise of

files (which is why COSCL should have an INQUIRE statement), the date and time, etc. I shall not discuss the syntax of it: variables and control structures have been around for years in programming languages and are well understood.

4.4.13 Networks

The time has come to say something about networks. Of course, the problems of command language standards arose long before networks were seriously considered, and have to be solved, networks or no networks. Evidently, while solving them we should keep extensions to networks in mind. A lot of work has been done to clarify these issues (D. Rayner, K. Hopper in [2]).

The main consideration when extending a command language for networking seems to be the ability to add another layer to the file naming scheme and extend the SUBMIT command with facilities for choosing a suitable computer. Luckily, this seems to be possible without complicating the rest of the standards process.

4.4.14 Utilities

Under this heading I group a number of commands which usually appear in command language proposals, but cannot in any sense be regarded as elementary commands. Typical such commands are:

APPEND (meaning concatenate two files), DIRECTORY (list a directory), ERASE (delete the contents of a file but not the file itself), PURGE (delete old cycles of a file), LIST, PRINT, PUNCH, COMPARE, COPY, MERGE, SORT, EDIT, and HELP.

You should be able to write and call all of these commands as ordinary programs in, say, Fortran. If you can't, there is some deficiency in the system proposed. There is no harm and some good in including them in a standard anyway, just to create a common library of the most useful utilities. Ideally, the committee proposing them should also take the trouble of actually defining the programs for them.

4.4.15 Defaults and Synonyms

Immediately after logon, a COSCL user has the opportunity to set defaults by the command DEFAULT. By this command he can change a number of defaults, primarily those for file handling, like default library, max-cycles. etc.

Further, there is a SYNONYM command, that allows the user to use shorter names for files and directories.

These special commands seem unnecessary; assignment to reference variables of the CCL type do the job in an easier and more general manner.

4.4.16 Debugging

COSCL proposes two commands for debugging, SUSPEND and TRACE. SUSPEND can stop the execution at interesting places and make the system wait for a user command. After a SUSPEND, execution can be restarted by RESUME. TRACE causes a printout when a variable is changed, a label reached, or a procedure entered.

I have some experience of these facilities in programming languages where they are a good thing to have. At first sight they seem slightly elaborate in a command language context, where sequences are apt to be fairly short and straight (i.e. no loops or branches). The problems to expect are that the user misunderstands the function of whole commands rather than being unable to follow assignments and flow of control.

4.4.17 Drop-through to Host Language

Occasionally, a user of a machine independent command language will have to execute a command in the local system's command language. This is known as 'drop-through to host language', and corresponds to the facility, common in high-level programming languages, of being able to call procedures in machine code.

COSCL explicitly provides a command HOST for this purpose. It is in the nature of things that applications of this command are either non-portable or not foreseeable − or we would have included the feature in question in the common command language.

103

4.5 DESIGN FOR A COMMON COMMAND LANGUAGE

Early in this chapter we set out a number of command language problems, as they were perceived when work started in the field. If you go back and check you will find they have all been treated by now. We are ready today to define machine independent command languages; in fact, as a conclusion of the discussions above, we may now see the outlines of a common command language as I would like to propose it. It turns out to be a quite eclectic proposal, combining elements of all the languages discussed above.

(1) A core command language
This contains only:
(a) A minimal logon/logoff with environment control as in COSCL.
(b) A facility for calling programs and system commands, and for transmitting file parameters together with the call. Compilation-linkage should be automatic, as in APL.

     The syntax of the call should indicate the direction of the file parameters in the manner of Unix, but otherwise it should be a standard call. The range of parameters should include lists and empty parameters, and it should be possible to retrieve the properties of a parameter from inside the called program, as in Kiwinet NCL and COSCL.

(c) There should be a facility for starting parallel sessions and routing their output to files, as in COSCL.

(2) Extensions to the core command language
(a) Simple variables at the command language level and command structures like IF-THEN-ELSE and loops (see CCL or any of the other current proposals).
(b) An exception handling facility as in CCL, i.e. an exception can be sensed after a subprogram call; if not sensed it will at once be passed on to the next higher block, eventually aborting the run.

(3) File handling
File handling facilities to be available from both the program language and command language level (see 5.9.2).

     The basic file concept would be that of Unix, i.e. a file would be a sequence of bytes; records would be delimited by a record separator character that is part of the file; space on the medium would be allocated automatically on demand.

The naming of files would be hierarchical in the manner of CCL. This hierarchical naming would be the main method of protection, supplemented by a facility to lock the file with keys for reading, writing and/or execution.

(4) Interfaces to special I/O
Description of text files that can function as standard interfaces to card I/O, tape I/O, graphics, etc.

(5) Interfaces to other computers in a network
The long-range goal is of course a completely transparent network which looks up the files you ask for and runs the job in the most economic machine that can handle it.

The short-range goal is an agreement on an extra level of hierarchic naming of files and computers, and facilities for transmitting files and jobs.

4.6 REFERENCES

[1] C. Unger (ed.); *Command Languages* (Proc. 1st IFIP Working Conference on Command Languages, Lund); North-Holland (publ.), 1975.

[2] R. A. Pocock (ed.), IFIP TC2 WG 2.7 Bulletin.

[3] D. Beech (ed.); *Command Language Directions* (Proc. 2nd IFIP Working Conference on Command Languages, Berchtesgaden); North-Holland (publ.), 1980.

[4] IFIP WG 2.7; Reference Model; 1983.

[5] British Computer Society Working Group on Job Control Language; *Journal of Development* JOD/78/119; November 1978.

[6] C. Gram *et al.*, Denmark's Technical University; Doc. ID 668, CCL-1, First Version of Common Command Language; Feb. 1977.

[7] K. Hopper, N. S. James, and P. C. Jenkins, Kiwinet system control and access, Report No. 34 — preliminary language specifications, Massey University Computer Centre, New Zealand, 1977.

[8] K. Hopper, N. S. James, and P. C. Jenkins, Report No. 35 — technical progress report, 1978.

[9] H. J. Kugler *et al.*, Project Nicola, Progress report No. 3, University of Dortmund, 1979.

[10] B. W. Kernighan and J. R. Mashey, The UNIX TM programming environment, in Software Practice and Experience, **9**, pp. 1–15, 1979.

[11] CODASYL Common Operating Systems Command Language Committee; COSCL *Journal of Development*, Version 2:0; May 1981.
[12] ANSI; OSCRL User Requirements (Rev. 2 of 1979-01-22), Subcommittee X3H1, 1979.

5

Towards better programming languages

All through this book we have been concerned with portability and standards. As long as we could move the programs from site to site we did not care too much whether they were easy to write and whether, once written, they could be safely run and maintained. Now we shall raise our sights a bit and discuss some ideas for better programming languages. Our goal might be to make programming so much easier that at least the majority of university people could write their own application programs as long as they were not too complicated.

I believe there will be more new programs written in the future than in the past. It is true that we shall gradually have access to very large and well-planned program libraries. But we already have very large, excellent libraries of ordinary books, and yet more books are written each year than ever before in history. Conditions and techniques change so fast that we seem unable to keep up. So I think programming will be an expanding activity for the foreseeable future. Proportionally, more of these programs will be written by end users who are not professional programmers; but even so, there will be plenty of work for the professionals as well.

Today's tools are in no way sufficient to support such large-scale user programming, and this is now being realised both inside and outside the computer world. The 1982 Physics Nobel Prize winner, Kenneth G. Wilson, writes: '. . . no large scale scientific computation can be checked to the point of scientific certainty, either by its author or another scientist. The reason for this is the unreadability, unpublishability, and evanescence of Fortran programs. . . . The credibility problems of scientific simulation could be eased by a proper replacement for Fortran. . . . Downgrade it to the level of an assembly language . . . this would allow continued access to Fortran subroutines and libraries and . . . highly optimised Fortran compilers' [1]. We shall also look into the question of whether programming languages really have to be different according to intended area of use or whether they might be unified into one or a few main languages — with suitable subsets, of course. We hear people argue that scientific and administrative ADP are getting to be more and more similar, and at the same time we hear there have to be many programming languages because there are so many types of applications. Who is right and who is wrong?

5.1 CAN THERE BE A COMMON PROGRAMMING LANGUAGE?

There are several ways of improving programming languages. One is to look at existing languages and compare their strong and weak points. Is there a necessary connection in the sense that a language must give up one thing in order to achieve another, or are these differences a matter of history and taste? Another way is to consider the daily problems of programming and try to think up ways of solving them. A third one is to try to approach a natural language problem statement, compare it with the resulting program, and try to pin down the reason why the program is so much longer and more difficult to understand.

It used to be argued that a language for technical-scientific ADP needed a formula-like syntax, a lot of facilities for arithmetic, a good procedure concept, and a library of mathematical functions. A language for administrative ADP, on the other hand, should have a syntax close to English, a good character handling facility, and a library with facilities like sort, merge and a report program generator. With time these original differences have narrowed down. It turned out that the procedure concept was a basic tool, quite as necessary in administrative as in scientific ADP. On the other hand, character handling was needed more and more by technical and scientific people to make results readable. In the case of linguists, text processing is in fact the main application. Libraries for different applications could be handled by the same basic tools. So, gradually the facilities have approached each other. New differences have grown up — for example, Cobol is now expanding its facilities for handling full screen terminals and queues of terminals working against a common data base — but no doubt these facilities will work their way into other languages in due course.

This seems to indicate that more or less the same tools can be used for widely different applications. Similar conclusions can be drawn by comparing languages like Fortran, Algol and APL, as is done below. Though intended for the same type of applications, they were widely different to start with and are now approaching each other.

It seems that there is no necessary difference between programming languages intended for different ranges of applications. So, for the rest of this chapter, I shall assume that all the features discussed and proposed could be intended for one language. Is there then a collision between desirable features? We shall soon see.

5.1.1 A Comparison of Programming Languages

I shall now show you a comparison I once made of those language features that, at one time or another, have made me tend to choose, or avoid, a certain language.

The languages compared were Fortran 66, NU-Algol (a local Algol 60, enhanced with string handling and some other features), and APL. They are presented in table form below. On one particular issue, data structures, all three languages considered below were equally bad, and you would have to choose Cobol if they were important enough.

Property	F66	Algol	APL
Widespread use	+		
Tolerance and efficiency	+		
Compatible with environment			−
Program form	(see below)		
Control structures	−	+	−
Long identifiers		+	+
Modularity	(see below)		
Compact function calls			+
Interface to operating system			+
Recursiveness		+	+
A character facility		+	+
Complete types			+
Declaration of variables	(see below)		
Dynamic arrays	−		+
Data structures	(see Cobol)		
Integrated types			+

I think most of the catchwords will be self-explanatory. They will all be explained in detail further on, but let me say a few words about them at once.

APL got minus marks for requiring a special keyboard and (at least on our system) for having a completely different file concept.

By 'complete types' I mean that the user can define a function of every type, and that every type has associated with it a set of constants.

By 'integrated types' I mean the merging of reals, integers and logicals into one type and the treatment of strings as character arrays.

You see at once that there are many differences between these languages, even though they were ostensibly designed for the same kind of applications, i.e. numerical computation. This underlines the point just made above that language differences are not caused by different application areas.

A second point, again reinforcing the argument above, is that many of the original differences are already disappearing. Fortran 77 has already got the IF-THEN-ELSE control structure and the character facility. Fortran 8X will have long identifiers, data structures, dynamic arrays and, I hope, some more of the good things listed above. Simula, regarded as a development of Algol, has data structures and complete types. It is also interesting to note that these languages are steadily increasing their range of use. Features originally intended for a certain class of applications proved useful in many other areas. Simula was once designed as a language for simulation. Today it is being promoted as a language for many applications, of which simulation is but one. APL started life as a mathematical notation. Today it is widely used for business applications.

5.1.2 Why I Use Fortran

We have all been exposed to a variety of programming languages and been faced with the necessity, or opportunity, to choose between them. (Sometimes, of course, there is no choice, because the task at hand is to expand or correct an existing program.)

I use Fortran 77 for most daily work. Since Fortran is often scorned and derided as an old-fashioned language, or even a disease, I feel I owe you an explanation to start with.

In many ways APL was the most interesting of the three languages I could choose from when I returned to active programming in 1980. It is a very clean language, whose content is almost wholly algorithmical. There is nothing to remind you of what machine you are using, and so it is easily the most portable of the three. Each procedure defined becomes a binary or unary operator, which gives an easy way of extending the language (this will be discussed under 'Procedure invocation' further on). Logicals, integers and reals are beautifully integrated in the number type. The easy switching between program editing and execution has been mentioned elsewhere. It is very nice to be able to type in '3+4' and have the system return '7'. In this respect APL is so easy a school kid can use it.

But APL has some glaring deficiencies as well. The special key-board is a well-known one, which is however reasonably easy to overcome by a hardware representation scheme. The right-to-left execution of formulas is more annoying, because it goes against ingrained habits and traps you all the time. It has been explained to me that an ordering of operators according to their traditional priority would be hard to combine with the facility that allows the user to define his own operators (though this has, in fact, been done, for example, by Algol 68). Even worse, an APL implementation usually cannot interface to the file standard and libraries used by other programming languages: APL is a world unto itself. This deficiency is often fatal, since it means you cannot write new APL programs to develop an existing Fortran application, and thus convert gradually to APL.

So, somewhat regretfully, I decided I could not use APL, and the choice boiled down to Fortran or Algol. I decided on Fortran — narrowly, since I had used Algol so much — for the following reasons.

It is an advantage to choose the language that is current at your computing centre, because you are then most likely to get help if something goes wrong. Even these days that mostly means Fortran because of its *widespread use*. If I were concerned with portability, that would again indicate Fortran, not because it is particularly portable, but because I can be reasonably sure to find it at the next site.

Next, consider Fortran's *tolerance*. By tolerance I mean things like the ability to use integers for non-standard purposes like pointers and Holleriths; the ability to by-pass type checking when calling a procedure; passing the start address of an array as a parameter, and similar features that nearly always make it possible for the user to achieve some new functionality that could not have been foreseen by the implementor and/or the standards committee. Since we shall always face new uses of computers and new situations, we shall always need this kind of loopholes. Fortran's tolerance is not costly, because it is based on its relatively simple procedure interface. This makes it easy to add new machine code subroutines to Fortran. Any improvement that jeopardises this advantage would be doubtful.

A main reason for Fortran's *efficiency* is again its simple procedure interface plus the ability to deduce all expression types within a program unit at compile time. This is not unduly restrictive, unless you happen to need dynamic data types.

So Fortran's strong points are efficiency, tolerance and widespread use. These points alone have guaranteed its existence for close to three decades. In other respects, Fortran 66 was a terrible language, and you can see from the table above that it comes out second or last in any other comparison of importance. I managed to avoid Fortran 66 for years. But the introduction of IF-THEN-ELSE and the CHARACTER type improved it enough to swing the balance, and make Fortran 77 quite reasonable for daily use. And Fortran's long history gives it a maturity that a new language may need a long time to achieve. For instance, many new languages lack the ERR=label feature in Fortran's READ. Every time there is an error in data, such a program aborts! This may seem like a detail; but these details make the difference between a workhorse and a nice toy.

5.2 SYNTAX

5.2.1 Choosing Syntax

I was a member at one time of a committee charged with producing an 'amalgam of Algol and Cobol'. (It was a European committee, and this happened in the days before transatlantic manufacturers had choked Algol to death by silence.) As was natural, the committee contained administrative and scientific people in roughly equal numbers.

We soon got into a spirited discussion on the relative merits of writing addition as 'A := A+B' or 'ADD B TO A'. So frank did the exchange of opinion become that the committee split in three at its first and only meeting: an Algol committee, a Cobol committee, and a long-range committee which was never heard from again. To my mind this incident proved that syntax is almost wholly a matter of tradition, background, and taste. Many people have since come to the same conclusion, which shows up in the way they always introduce a new facility by saying: 'The syntax is illustrative only'. Nobody wants his ideas thrown out because they were served with the wrong sauce.

Happily, it seems that we can put almost any syntax into any language. It is a question of changing the input to the compiler.

Take a simple example: the IF-THEN-ELSE construct. It was in Algol for 17 years before it was accepted into Fortran. It first appeared in pre-processors and was in fact easy to add to Fortran. Once it was accepted into the language, it caused no trouble. The same will be the case with long identifiers, when they come. The only problems you are likely to have with syntax are those of continuity and conflicting usage. If you have always used end-of-line as statement delimiter, you cannot use semicolon instead, because that will make old programs incompatible with the new compiler. If you have used full stops to delimit reserved words (.EQ., .AND.) you cannot easily use them between fields in structured names. But if you start defining a new language from scratch, you can have almost any syntax you wish, at marginal cost.

Having said that people's taste in syntax is a matter of tradition and background, and that syntax can be chosen quite freely, I certainly do not mean to imply that the choice is unimportant. Bad syntax is a daily problem. As I said before, the absence of IF-THEN-ELSE and strings made me avoid Fortran 66 for years and stick to Univac Algol. I like being able to read my programs.

The methods used for choosing syntax could certainly be improved. A recent paper made comparative time studies of the effect of competing control structures. This is a fresh departure that could profitably be used on many activities in programming. It is an unpleasant reality that we programmers who largely work in the field of office automation have to accept — and do accept! — such mediocre tools for ourselves. A conventional time studies man would probably tear his hair if he saw programmers in action.

On the whole, I rather like Fortran's program form, though it is a bit old-fashioned. I like using end-of-line as the normal end-of-statement, and I love Fortran's comment facility: it is so easy to use that it positively encourages you to comment the program. To my mind APL's form is too compact, and if I were to use APL extensively, I would probably introduce more words instead of symbols for the operators, but, as I said, that is a matter of taste.

Fortran 77 already has IF-THEN-ELSE, so that is no longer an issue. Fortran 8X is getting DO-REPEAT and CASE. Next on the list is the DO-WHILE and REPEAT-UNTIL. It is a good thing to have both, so that there is a natural choice of construct according as the minimum number of executions of the loop is zero or one. But I regard these improvements as marginal compared to IF-THEN-ELSE. The only thing I really need over Fortran's present syntax is DO-REPEAT and *long identifiers*.

It may seem exaggerated to let the availability of long identifiers influence the choice of language; but it really is an important issue. Once you have got used to being able to have long identifiers, you miss them badly if you can't have them. It is not that I usually write very long identifiers. I try to keep them short whenever they can be abbreviated in a normal manner. But it is a relief not to have to abbreviate identifiers out of any semblance of readability, and to be able to differentiate between almost identical identifiers. The fact that a recent questionnaire among Fortran users drew such limited response to this feature (which was nevertheless included in Fortran 8X) shows how important it is not to get bogged down in any one language. Had the questionnaire been directed at people who had started out with other languages and then been forced into Fortran, the response would have been loud and clear.

Let me summarise the discussion so far:

— Almost all useful ideas can be unified in one language.
— It is a good thing to build on Fortran.
— Syntax can be chosen quite freely to suit the user.

If you can accept these rather controversial tenets for the time being, we can now go through the issues one by one. At each step we shall consider what features we wish to have in a future programming language starting from Fortran. We shall investigate which features collide, which of them carry a cost, and how can we avoid paying that cost when we do not need it. We shall start out by considering procedure calls.

5.3 PROCEDURE CALLS

This is an exciting and important topic. There are a number of schools of thought on this and we shall want to discuss them all and try to weigh them against each other. We have here both matters of syntax and facilities, but we shall treat the whole complex as one topic.

Before we start, let me clear up a point of terminology: I shall use the word 'subprogram' in its Fortran sense, i.e. meaning the union of subroutines, functions and block data subprograms. I shall use the word 'procedure' for subroutines and functions. The words 'argument' and 'parameter' will be used as synonyms.

5.3.1 The Classical Interface

The classical Fortran interface has two important properties:

(1) Subprograms can be compiled independently.
(2) Very simple information is passed when the subprogram is called.

All our three languages are different in this respect: Fortran has independent compilation, Algol has dependent compilation, and APL has interpretation. The idea behind independent compilation is that you can recompile a single procedure if you change it, and make a new linkage to the other program parts without recompiling them. An Algol program has to be recompiled whole every time. An APL procedure is interpreted during execution so it can in fact have a different effect in the same session, depending on where it is called from. Independent compilation is, of course, the fastest, but the independently compiled subprograms do not always work together, as every experienced Fortran programmer knows. One of the most common and frustrating experiences in a Fortran environment is to have working program systems blow up because somebody changed a few common variables somewhere in the library.

Separate compilation is not costly − in fact, the opposite is true. The Algol principle of baking all procedures into one vast pie has the double disadvantage of preventing you from getting a good overview *and* forcing you to recompile everything if there is one error.

Strictly speaking, the Fortran standard does not mention independent compilation. It does not mention compilation at all, speaking only of 'the Fortran processor'. Independent compilation is so to speak an implementation tradition, made possible by certain restrictions on the language. An important one is the syntax of the COMMON statement: A list of COMMON variables must be repeated whole in each program unit where any of its variables is used. Further, since we cannot assume any knowledge of the subprograms called, the call alone must be a sufficient interface. This problem, however, appears even in a joint-compilation language like Algol 60, since one can call a procedure that is a formal parameter and thus unknown at compile time. Therefore, your system must either allow all parameter to be checked at run time, or allow you to make auxiliary 'declarations' explaining the properties of called subprograms within the calling program.

117

It used to be that the call of a Fortran procedure passed very little information for each argument. A memory address to a variable, an array element or a working storage position was enough. Part of Fortran's tolerance came from this: it was easy to plug an assembler procedure into that simple interface and no checks for argument matches were made either at compile or run time.

The classic interface required the actual parameters to match the formal parameters exactly in number and type. This can be quite tedious when there are many parameters, some of which are used infrequently. It is unduly restrictive when you want to write a procedure with a variable number of parameters, or allow parameters of different types to appear in the same position.

5.3.2 Variable number of arguments

The first improvement that comes to mind is to allow procedures with a variable number of arguments. The idea is formulated as a formal proposal below. The ideas in this proposal are based on the *Journal of Development* of the CODASYL COSCLC (ref. [11] of Chapter 4).

> The final dummy argument of a procedure may be an ellipsis (. . .). There may be none, one, or more than one associated actual argument.
>
> Within the procedure, the type of each argument may be retrieved by the character-valued function TYPE.
>
> TYPE(ARGUM(n))   'n' is the ordinal number of the actual argument, counting only those arguments that are associated with the ellipsis. A string specifying the type of the argument is returned. If no argument with this number exists, blank is returned.

The actual argument value or name can be retrieved by the following expression:

> type(ARGUM(n))   'type' may be REAL, INTEGER, etc. (any type that is defined in the program unit) and must be the same as the type returned by the call TYPE (ARGUM(n)). 'n' is the ordinal number of the argument. The expression can be used as a reference to the argument or to return a value to it.

(Note: this proposal, taken directly from COSCL, will have to be modified slightly in syntax to avoid collision with Fortran's existing conversion routines, and with future data structure constants.)

Example:

```
     REAL FUNCTION ADD (. . .)
     ADD = 0.0
     N = 1
10   T = TYPE(ARGUM(N))
     IF (T.NE.'REAL') RETURN
     ADD = ADD+REAL(ARGUM(N))
     N = N+1
     GO TO 10
     END
```

Extension 1: Conversion is forced, if 'type' is different from the type of the actual argument.

Extension 2: The TYPE function may be applied to any dummy argument to check the existence and type of the associated actual argument.

To implement this, we shall enhance the interface by transmitting the following information for each parameter:

— the type of the entity
— the address of the entity or its 'dope vector', and, once in the call,
— either the number of parameters or an end-of-parameter signal.

(A dope vector is a set of values which allows the system to handle a complex entity; for example, the starting address and bounds of an array.)

Once this is done, all the requested features are possible:

— The type of a parameter can be sensed from within the subprogram. An automatic type check, and conversion, is possible.
— A parameter can be left out of the parameter sequence.
— The number of parameters can be variable.

5.3.3 Form of the Call

A number of syntaxes have been used or proposed to describe procedure calls, and we shall now have a look at those, including the classical one of Fortran. I shall skip the word CALL in the syntax, since the discussion concerns both subroutines and functions. CALL is a redundant word anyway, and specific to Fortran, a rare example of 'syntactic sugar' in that language.

(1) proc-name (param-1, param-2, . . . param-n)

This is the classical method. It is cumbersome to write and read if there are very many parameters.

(2) proc-name (keywd-a=param-a, keywd-b=param-b, . . .)

This is a more convenient form of (1), where parameters may be written in an arbitrary order and identified by their keywords. To be useful, this form must allow you to leave out a parameter and have a default value supplied for it.

> Example (cf. Kiwinet NCL in Chapter 4):
> Call: WHATSIT(5,TEXT="STOP",INT1);
> Meaning;   WHATSIT(5,FILEA,FILEB,"STOP",INT1);

(3) result $\longleftarrow$ param-a proc-name param-b

This is the APL method. It is very elegant when applicable, but it is inherently limited to two input parameters and one result parameter. If there are more parameters, you may be able to handle them with arrays and other structured variables, but the resultant notation may no longer be so natural.

> Example:
> Call: OUTTEXT X FORMATTED_BY 'F5.2'
> Meaning: OUTTEXT(FORMATTED_BY(X, 'F5.2'))

Roughly speaking, method 2 is good for procedures with many parameters, and method 3 for procedures with few parameters. Both try to achieve an easier and more natural call by different methods. Method 2 tries to cut down on unnecessary parameters and make the rest easy to remember. Method 3 tries to achieve a more natural word order and do away with parentheses: if you have a function FORMATTED_BY with two parameters, a value and a format, it is obviously more natural to have the verb between the parameters rather than in front of them. If I had to choose between them, I would (narrowly) choose 2, though 3 is more elegant. I would do so

(a) because 3 is limited to two input parameters and its word order is not always the natural one,
(b) because 2 can be enhanced by the method below.

It might not, in fact, be necessary to choose — a sophisticated compiler could conceivably handle both methods — but that would perhaps be too elaborate.

(4) (param-1) proc-name (param-2, . . . param-n)

This is a sort of compromise between (1) and (3), allowing you to leave out the word CALL and place the procedure name wherever it is natural in the parameter sequence. It can obviously be enhanced with the keyword facility, and would then make a rather nice call mechanism as far as the syntax of the call is concerned.

With this mechanism the method 3 example would become:

OUTTEXT((X) FORMATTED_BY ('F5.2'))

which differs from the APL example only by having several parentheses in it.

While we are at it, let us note that the Unix pipeline facility is also a way of calling procedures elegantly (though hardly general enough for all-round use):

Unix:	who / grep joe / wc
Fortran:	wc(grep('joe',who))
APL:	wc 'joe' grep who

where we may think of 'grep' as a two argument function and 'wc' as a one argument subroutine.

Having chosen method 4, we must now consider some way of separating those actual parameters which correspond to the list of formal arguments and should be treated as positional and keyword arguments from those that correspond to the ellipsis (. . .) and are variable number arguments. Further, we must consider how to implement keyword arguments. Are we to convert the keyworded call to a complete call? If so, we would need a description of the called subprogram at compile time. And that, as we have seen earlier, is not in general possible. We might supply descriptions manually, which is tedious. Or again, we can handle it by parameter passing; you may transmit the keyword as a separate parameter at run time, signalling 'the next parameter is to be attached to the keyword transmitted now'. A fourth possibility is to use the variable number of arguments facility to transmit keywords. This minimises the amount of enhancement needed, but means you have to organise the procedure so that the frequently used parameters are transmitted first in a fixed order and the infrequent ones transmitted after that, each one preceded by a character string that the procedure treats as a keyword.

I think the issue is close. I am prepared to settle for the variable number of arguments facility plus the free placing of the procedure name. Those two features are easy to implement and would be a great improvement over today's rigid call syntax.

Programmers are never satisfied. With free operator definition around the corner, people are already discussing the possibility of defining the same operator several times, each time with a new result type. In Algol 68 and Ada, this is known as 'overloading' and creates a generic operator, i.e. an operator that takes its type from its arguments the way plus (+) has always done and the generic functions do in Fortran 77.

5.3.4 The INTENT Declaration and the Environment Unit

I have earlier been a proponent of an INTENT declaration, and this is the place to discuss it briefly.

An INTENT declaration is an addition to the parameter specifications of a procedure. It tells us whether the parameter is intended to input a value to the procedure, return a result from it, or both.

The motivation for it is sound. It is intended to make it possible for a compiler to check whether the flow of computation in a program unit makes sense, i.e. that each variable is first initialised or input, then possibly changed, and finally used in further computations or output. If any variable falls outside this 'life cycle', something is wrong. The variable may be superfluous, its name may have been misspelt, or there is some logical flaw in the program.

Example:

```
READ(5,*)  X, Y, Z
U = X+Y
V = U/Z
WRITE (6,*) V
```

In this example, the flow of computation is easy to follow, because there are no procedure calls. X, Y and Z are input, U is an intermediate result using X and Y, V is a final result using U and Z, and it is output. All variables are assigned to and used. The program makes sense.

Now suppose Z was misspelt as 2 in the computation of V. The program is still formally correct. But a human reader would wonder why Z was read in and never used. The break in the computation flow would point to an error.

This kind of analysis is much harder to perform if the program contains many procedure calls. A lot of the time used when analysing other people's programs (or your own old programs) is spent tracing the flow of computation. An INTENT declaration is intended to ease this work; it could make it possible to perform it by a program.

Now for the arguments against. First of all, it cannot be made mandatory in Fortran, because that would invalidate all existing programs. Second, we have the usual problem of making all procedures available to the compiler, including the bothersome ones that are formal parameters and thus unknown until run time. Third, we have just adopted the variable number of parameters feature. The intent of those parameters can hardly be analysed by a program, though the human reader would usually understand or be helped out by a comment. Fourth, there are a number of other reasons why a computation flow analysis can not be made water-proof. Last, but not least, I would like to see the intent by looking at the call alone (as Unix allows me to do). Things will probably improve when we get data structures and complete types, because we shall often be able to compress all output into one structured function value and let this be the only output from the procedure.

Even considering all these arguments, I think the intent declaration could be helpful (and Fortran 8X is now borrowing it from Ada in the form of IN OUT). I can imagine future programmers building up and maintaining an Environment Unit for each large project. This would contain the headings of all subprograms belonging to the current program with some extra information on arguments and common entities, against which all subprogram calls could be checked. Both the creation of the E.U. and the checking against it could be done automatically, with some manual intervention in close cases. A library of procedures would form another E.U. which the programmer could merge with his own E.U. if he used the library. Checking out the interplay between procedures and keeping up with changes in it is a recurring task for the active programmer. A degree of formalisation of that task would not hurt.

5.3.5 Recursive Procedures

Recursion is one of those few features that *are* tied to specific applications. Three groups of applications come to mind: the computation of recursively defined mathematical functions, the analysis of sentences in linguistics, and the analysis of statements by a compiler (the two latter applications are of course closely related, both being language analyses).

Once you have an application where recursion is needed, you will find that it is hard to be without. It is not easy to simulate a recursive procedure by a non-recursive one. All variables have to be replicated for each level of recursion, so simple variables must be converted into one-dimensional arrays, one-dimensional arrays into two-dimensional, and so on. If the recursive call occurs within an expression, the expression has to be broken down in simple components so that intermediate results are explicitly stored in variables and replicated too. Some special machine code trick has to be found to store and use the successive return addresses. In addition, there is the problem of knowing exactly which procedures will be called recursively. Recursion is not always direct, but can occur in chains, the procedure A calling B, that calls C that comes back and calls A. So at present, if you get this kind of application, I suggest you try some other language than Fortran, for instance APL or Simula.

Now recursion is actually being proposed for Fortran 8X. Since a general recursiveness has a definite cost in terms of efficiency, a new procedure interface and decreased tolerance, it is planned to declare RECURSIVE only those procedures that in fact need recursion. In that case there is no extra cost for the other procedures; in effect we have introduced a subset of non-recursive procedures. We are still left with the problem of knowing which procedures need to be recursive. Whether recursion will actually work well with the other features of Fortran is still an open question; I have my doubts but admit I have not been able to produce a convincing example. I hope I am wrong.

5.3.6 Shared Variables

The time has now come to consider the sharing of variables between different program units in a program. The classic Fortran device is the COMMON area. It is considered a bit crude for two reasons. First, the COMMON area has to have the same (unqualified) name in all program units where it appears. This may be restrictive on the user if he is using a package, and there may be collision between packages. Second, all variables in the COMMON area up to the last one used must be declared. This means once a variable has come into a COMMON block it is dangerous to take it away. On the other hand, Algol and APL cannot make variables in packages accessible to the user at all. Simula is much better, making variables accessible by qualified names. It does mean a certain amount of extra compile-time or run-time work, and the end of separate compilation, but it is probably worth the cost.

USE and BUNDLE in Fortran 8X solve these problems well.

While I am at it, I would like the ability to reach systems variables to be included in the language. One may wish to have special naming conventions for these (e.g. they should all contain a $ sign). At one time or other, I have felt the need to reach:

— remaining time for user,
— date and wall clock time,
— margin control variables for the system printer, and
— user and project identification.

5.3.7 Dynamic Compilation

In APL a procedure can be edited by another procedure and then executed. This can be very useful at times, since it means a dynamic changing of the program text.

I tried once to formulate a text to add to the Fortran standard to make this possible in Fortran too. Rather amusingly, I realised it could not be done, because there is nothing in the Fortran standard to prevent you from dynamically modifying a subroutine. You could OPEN a file called 'SUB', WRITE in it, and immediately execute CALL SUB(. . .). It would not work, of course, because SUB has not been recompiled. But it is a perfectly logical interpretation of the program, and it is not ruled out by the standard, which does not use the concept of compilation at all. If it does not work in any normal Fortran processor today, it is not because the construct is against the standard. It is a matter of a massive implementation tradition.

5.3.8 On Side Effects

Now and then when you read a computer language proposal, you will stumble over a sentence prohibiting 'unwanted side effects' of commands or functions. If you have never tangled with this issue, you will probably wonder why this had to be pointed out, nod agreement, and read on without giving it a second thought. But the matter is not quite as simple, and I shall devote a few paragraphs to discussing it.

The side effects issue was fought in the early 1960s between two groups of Algol 60 implementors, let us call them the optimisers and the orthodox. A side effect happens when a function changes a variable outside of itself directly, i.e. not through a formal parameter. A famous example is the following one, taken from an Algol 60 course and published in the Algol Bulletin [2]. The original is to the left and a corresponding piece of Fortran code to the right.

real procedure Sneaky(z);	REAL FUNCTION SNEAKY(Z)
value z; *real* z;	COMMON W
begin Sneaky := z+(z−2)↑2;	SNEAKY = Z+(Z−2)**2
W := z+1	W = Z+1
end Sneaky	END

As you can see, Sneaky computes a function value of z and then changes the global variable W; this is the side effect. Consequently, the value of, say, W*Sneaky(z) could be different from Sneaky(z)*W. In the first case the old value of W might be used, in the second case the new value of W. An optimising compiler might be forgiven for evaluating the first case by first computing Sneaky(z) and then multiplying by W, thus inadvertently using the new W.

The orthodox wanted to fix the order of evaluation of primaries from left to right in order to have the effect of such programs exactly defined. This meant saving W in a stack before starting on Sneaky(z). Since they were using stacks anyhow in order to handle recursive procedures, they did not care about the loss of efficiency involved. The optimisers went to the opposite extreme. They wanted to prohibit functions from changing global variables. A function would then only depend on its parameters and a lot of optimisation would be possible. A number of people, including myself, preferred to have the text stand and let the effect of these cases remain undefined.

Of course, the Sneaky example was an unhappy choice because it did not show a useful application of side effects. A much better one was published in the next issue of the bulletin. But the damage was done. Side effects were roundly condemned as tricky coding and the stigma remains to this day.

It is interesting to note how Fortran handles the issue. Side effects are in general permitted, as the example above shows. As the example also shows, the variable concerned must be in COMMON, so at least there are no inadvertent side effects. The Fortran 77 standard further says: 'The execution of a function reference in a statement may not alter the value of any other entity within the statement in which the function reference appears. The execution of a function reference in a statement may not alter the value of any entity in common that affects the value of any other function reference in that statement', Thus the expression W*SNEAKY(Z) is prohibited (= not defined) in Fortran. And this is probably the best way to handle the issue.

There are some very similar cases where you want to be careful. Suppose you define the functions NEXTREAL and NEXTINT whose values are taken from two different fields in the next record of an input file. Each call reads a record and advances the file. This side effect is not transmitted through COMMON, but has the same effect of making NEXTREAL ( )+NEXTINT ( ) different from NEXTINT ( )+NEXTREAL ( ). Another example is a function RANF giving a random number. This function must have a SAVEd variable somewhere that is used and changed by each call and ensures that the next random number in some sequence is used. Thus RANF ( )+SIN(RANF ( )) differs from SIN(RANF ( ))+RANF ( ). A third case is the function that gives you wall clock time. In this case the side effect is the inexorable march of time (and the consequent updating of some counter in the operating system). But again we have a case where the value of a function varies irrespective of its parameters, in fact without its having parameters at all. And with this I think we have penetrated this issue enough. Now you know what you are doing when you condemn side effects.

5.3.9 The Main Program as a Command Language Subroutine

The Fortran main program is normally called from the operating system. In relation to the OS, the main program may be regarded as a subroutine. The files known to the operating system may be regarded as actual parameters in the call of the Fortran main program. The logical units within the main program are in effect formal parameters, becoming associated with the actual files.

Consider a very simple program ERASE, intended to erase the contents of a sequential file. (I chose ERASE because it is often – unnecessarily – introduced as a primitive function in command language proposals.) The call of ERASE (in some simple common command language) and its Fortran 77 code might be:

```
ERASE #1=MYFILE        OPEN (1)
                       ENDFILE 1
                       END
```

Call and code of a simple program

In addition to the Fortran program, there has to be some command language information identifying the program as ERASE, compiling it, etc.

This works, though the parameter '#1=MYFILE' looks slightly silly. (It is high time to phase out unit numbers from Fortran.) Some reflection shows that since a Fortran main program acts as a subroutine called by the OS, it ought to have a heading with a formal parameter whose name may — but need not — be used as a keyword in the call, say:

```
ERASE F=MYFILE         PROGRAM ERASE(F)
    or                 UNIT F
ERASE MYFILE           OPEN(F)
                       ENDFILE F
                       END
```

Call and code in revised Fortran

(In this case we do not wish to open the file by an OPEN statement in the Fortran program:

```
OPEN(1,FILE='MYFILE')
```

because then we would have to rewrite the program every time it is used for a new file. The use of a file name in an OPEN statement is useful when, and only when, it is always the same file, or if the file name is somehow generated by the Fortran program.)

If we want ERASE to be able to erase several files in one call, the Fortran program must contain some mechanism for retrieving an array of names supplied as a parameter, or for handling a variable number of parameters, as proposed above in the section on procedure calls.

The future common command languages are certain to include facilities for passing other parameters than files: integers, strings, etc. The parameter passing facility should thus not be limited to the type UNIT.

Speaking specifically of Fortran, I propose the PROGRAM statement to have the alternate form:

PROGRAM name (argument-list)

where each entry in 'argument-list' is an argument passed from the environment that calls the main program.

The rules for such arguments should be as for procedure arguments, where applicable.

5.4 DATA ENTITIES

5.4.1 'Complete Types'

Before we start discussing desirable types and their properties, I should like to formulate the principle of *type completeness*.

It is really rather trivial. Any data type that is introduced in a programming language should be complete, in the sense that it should be possible to declare not only variables but also functions of that type, and there should be constants of the type. (In the case of Fortran, it is more or less necessary also to have a format corresponding to the type.) APL is perfect in this respect, whereas Fortran had, and has, serious deficiencies: arrays can be declared, but not used as functions and constants; the old Hollerith type had only a format and constants, but could not be used in declarations; now strings have declarations and constants but cannot be used as functions. This is particularly exasperating, since there actually exist implicit functions of type CHARACTER – but the *user* may not create any!

This brings me to a second general principle, which – for want of a better term – I call the principle of *implementation economy*. It says that if a certain feature is present in the language processor, the user should be allowed to reach it.

Another example is the conversion between strings and variable names. When I use name-directed input, I can enter 'X = 3.14' as an input record and the processor finds X and stores 3.14 in X. So evidently the processor can read the string 'X' and convert it to the machine address of X. In effect, the processor must have a dictionary of the program unit's variables, at least of those mentioned in the input list. So why am I not, as a user, allowed to use this facility too:

VAR_CALLED('X') = 3.14

Once the subprogram carries a dictionary, that would make it possible to access all variables of a subprogram unit from the calling program. I admit it could be a dangerous practice, but at least it would be a way to implement the USE of Fortran 8X without dependent compilation.

A third example is subprogram calls with a variable number of parameters. The READ and WRITE systems procedures have this facility, so obviously the processor can handle it. Why cannot the user have the same freedom in his procedures?

Now let us get back to the principle of completeness, and look at another aspect of it. If a data type is arrayed, it is vital that its dimensions be retrievable. The newly introduced type CHARACTER in Fortran has this property, in the form of the intrinsic function LEN(string) which returns the length in characters of its argument. The current array proposal for Fortran 8X has also recently become complete on all counts.

5.4.2 Dynamic Arrays

We now come to one of the most troublesome deficiencies in programming languages: the lack of dynamic arrays. It is a daily problem, and it affects not only your own programs. Many times when external program packages blow up and you are helpless to do anything about it, lack of dynamic space is behind it. I shall therefore discuss the alternatives quite thoroughly.

As we mentioned earlier, Fortran 66 has completely static arrays. It is the same with Fortran 77. We may call this level 1.

In Algol 60 variable bound arrays can be created in subprograms but not saved. This we shall call level 2. This scheme is fairly cheap to implement, but does not give enough facilities: you must compute the array bounds before entering any block; thus you cannot reallocate the storage while working on the arrays.

What is needed additionally is a facility to create and to reallocate storage anywhere in the program unit. A frequent example in practice is that a program starts its work by reading in some arrays from an input unit. These arrays, and possibly others that are computed from them later on, need dynamic storage allocation.

If we restrict ourselves to a stacking scheme, this can still be done quite cheaply (level 3). By a stacking scheme I mean that an array can increase its size only if it is the last active array in the stack: any arrays created later must be dropped first.

Level 4, the most ambitious one, gives us complete freedom to change the size of any array any time. To implement this means the running system must move the arrays back and forth. Therefore this level gives slower execution than the other ones. This, it seems, is the level proposed for Fortran 8X.

Now what is the pay-off between memory utilisation, speed, safety and ease of use at those different levels of dynamic-ness?

At level 1 we get the highest speed, since all array bounds and addresses are fixed at compile time. On the other hand, there is a loss of space every time the array bounds are set too high. When they are set too low, the program does not work (which you may, or may not, become aware of). You will probably have an option of switching on a check for subscripts out of bounds, which will give you security at the cost of speed.

At level 2 you will still have almost the same speed as at level 1. The system has to compute the start address of each array anew when it is created, but the time lost is usually marginal compared to the time it takes to process the individual elements of the array. The storage utilisation should be a lot better, since the array sizes can often be appropriate to the current execution. The risk of malfunction will also be less.

At level 3 we shall be able to get the right size also for arrays that the program reads from outside. Thus there is another clear improvement in storage utilisation and safe functioning. There is no extra penalty in speed this time, since the mechanism for computing addresses was already introduced at level 2.

At level 4, finally, we get optimum storage utilisation and safe functioning. Every array can always get its right size. Speed is seemingly lost, since the shuffling of arrays back and forth takes time. But, and this is a very important but, this shuffling does not have to begin until the storage is full. Then it does take time, but the alternative would have been to abort the program. And it is evidently more economical to have the run completed at a slower speed, than having wasted the work already done.

To my mind, the issue is not even close. The more dynamic the arrays, the better will the programs work and utilise storage. Appreciable loss of speed will not take place until the storage is full — and then the alternative to a slow-down would have been to abort the program.

Before we leave arrays, I would like to mention a recent idea. Could we have arrays that can be reshaped dynamically, as in APL? It seems quite easy to implement, since it just means changing the dope vector without touching or moving the elements. As far as I can see, it can be done dynamically in a program, as often as you wish; there is no objection to the same array appearing with a different number of subscripts in the same program unit.

5.4.3 Variable Types

We have seen Fortran acquire a new data type BIT and declared precision of REALs, so it now has BIT, LOGICAL, INTEGER, REALs of various kinds and CHARACTER. Each of these has a number of associated intrinsic operations, and we might well wonder if there is some way of consolidating these types and operations.

Guided by APL which has only NUMERIC and CHARACTER, we shall begin by merging the classical types, LOGICAL, INTEGER and REAL.

The merging of LOGICAL and INTEGER is fairly easy. As in APL, we shall simply consider .TRUE. to equal 1, and .FALSE. to equal 0. Thus the value of 3.EQ.3 is 1, 3.EQ.4 is 0, 3.LT.5 is 1, etc. Instead of 'IF(I.EQ.J) N=N+1', we can write 'N=N+(I.EQ.J)' (whether that is an improvement is open to discussion). The operations .EQV. and .NEQV. can be eliminated in favour of the ordinary .EQ. and .NE., since they accomplish the same thing. All this could be done without merging the type declarations. The merging of declarations can be done in the manner of Pascal, which allows you to define a type LOGICAL as a special case of INTEGER having the range 0 to 1:

LOGICAL = 0 .. 1

The next manoeuvre, of merging INTEGER and REAL into one type, let us call it NUMERIC, is also deceptively easy. To a great extent they are merged in Fortran already, since INTEGERs and REALs can be mixed in arithmetic expressions. But a complete merge would mean that they could also be used interchangeably, e.g. in procedure calls. We can presume that the values would be stored in such a manner that the system could distinguish dynamically between reals of different precision and between exact values (integers) and approximate values (reals). The type of operation and of the result could then also be determined dynamically, based on the types of the operands, much as it is done at compile time in present-day Fortran. Or all storing and computation could be in double precision, as is the case in some APL implementations. It is safe and convenient, but expensive; if this became a standard it would, however, be fairly easy to build hardware for it.

The next obvious step is to eliminate the difference between LOGICAL and BIT. It is easy to see that LOGICAL is in effect the same as BIT*1. The operations on LOGICAL and BIT are the same; .BAND. corresponds to .AND., .BOR. to .OR., etc. There is no reason for having different names. So BIT and LOGICAL alone are also easy to merge into one.

However, merging BIT and NUMERIC is more difficult. There is no easy way to extend the meaning of .AND., .OR., etc. to arbitrary numbers. The best one could do would be to extend the logical operations to non-negative integers, which are easy to convert to bit strings. Thus 5 .AND. 6 would become 4 (B101 .AND. B110 = B100), 3 .OR. 4 would become 7, etc. Conversely, the arithmetic operations on non-negative integers could be applied to bit strings: B10+B100= B110. (We could not extend them to negative numbers, because here we would run into the many different schemes of representing negative numbers by bits.) This would leave us with two overlapping subtypes within the NUMERIC/BIT type, one consisting of BIT, LOGICAL and non-negative integers, the other one consisting of LOGICAL, INTEGER and REAL. Within the first subtype, logical operations would be applicable; within the second, arithmetic operations and inequality operations. The equal and not-equal operators would apply all over the merged type with a question mark, perhaps, for real numbers.

While restricting the domain of certain operations within a type may seem odd at first, it is really not in contrast to what we are used to in the world of pen-and-paper processing. We shall discover this when we think of merging all the other types with CHARACTER. Before we discuss that, we may note that merging BIT and NUMERIC in an inefficient manner is pointless, since BIT, more than any other type, is an optimising feature tied to special applications (real-time processes, raster graphics).

All data types can be expressed in terms of characters. This is how we think of values when they are outside computers. We are of course vaguely aware of the fact that addition can be applied to '2' and '4', but not to the strings 'A' and 'B', and this causes us no mental problems.

It could be very interesting to implement a character-only package in Fortran just to experiment with it. You would soon discover, for example, that the simple .GT. operator has one meaning when applied to numbers and another when applied to general strings; e.g. the following relations hold:

4711 > 26	and	'4711' >	'26'
4711 > 62	but	'4711' <	'62'
62 > 26	and	'62' >	'26'
−26 > −62	but	'−26' <	'−62'

In fact, it is disputable whether the same operator should be used here; we might well want to distinguish string compare from number compare. In the same manner we ought to distinguish assign to integer from assign to real, since assign to integer can force a truncation or rounding, or rather always use explicit conversion to integer, so assignment always assigns the right hand expression unchanged.

In a package like this different schemes for real precision could also be tried, and also the exception handling proposed below.

This is the place to point out the need for dynamic length of character strings. The case for this is very similar to the one made for dynamic arrays: better memory utilisation, safety and user convenience, but the cost in terms of slower speed is not so marginal in the case of strings. Since strings are on the average smaller than arrays, a program can contain many more of them, and there may be a lot of shuffling, as they grow and jostle for space. But again, if you know how long each string at most can be, you are still free to give it that length from the start. You can program as efficiently as your knowledge permits; but dynamic strings would give you a new option when memory is scarce and you do not know which strings are going to need it most.

It is easy to protest that such a scheme would be enormously inefficient. But remember then that this is the way Cobol is defined; and, inefficient or not, it is the most widespread high level language in the world. Cobol is defined completely in terms of characters and decimal numbers. There exists the COM-PUTATIONAL facility to speed up numeric computation. It is clearly labelled as an optimising feature, and its use is receding with cheaper machines and increased awareness of portability. So, in this respect, Cobol was far ahead of all other high level languages.

It might well be argued that characters are the natural way, in fact the only way, for a human to think of symbols. In a non data processing environment we represent numbers and words in the same way, as character groups; we recognise numbers only by their being chosen from a limited character set and we do not consciously 'convert' or 'decode' them before applying numerical operations to them. (The only entities used in data processing that we do not spontaneously think of as character groups are pictures.) The reason we do not work the same way in technical data processing is that keeping numbers in their character form and operating on them that way is inefficient, as we just said. But this is mostly a result of the way we build our hardware (other hardware schemes were tried and discarded – perhaps prematurely – in the 1950s.)

I rather hesitate to propose that all the Fortran types actually should be merged into one. But I would like to summarise the discussion above into the following concrete proposals.

(1) Establish CHARACTER as the basic, stand-alone data type, and treat the other types as openly declared optimisation aids.
(2) Treat LOGICAL as a special case of INTEGER.
(3) Merge operators which work the same. That is, merge .BAND. with .AND., .EQV. with .EQ., etc.
(4) Distinguish operators that do not work the same. This applies, for example, to relational operators on numbers contra strings. For the same reason, require explicit conversion from real to integer on assignment.

5.4.4 Data Structures

Now and then it happens that you wish to combine data into structures. You may have a number of objects, each of them described by a group of variables. You want to be able to treat such a group of variables as a whole, while retaining access to the individual variables. This is achieved by using data structures. Data structures appeared early in Cobol, where they are used, for example, to describe the structure of file records.

Data structures, in combination with the facility for declaring new operators and adding new domains for existing ones, are also useful for creating new data types. If we did not already have the COMPLEX type in Fortran, it could be created as a data structure.

Present proposals for data structures in Fortran 8X look very promising. There is no trade-off to speak of – they are perfectly implementable in Fortran. Then why did they take so long?

Here we come into tradition. Structured data came early in Cobol, because administrative ADP typically handles records containing different values attached to an individual. But now we see that they are actually needed in scientific ADP too. So there is another point to the side that claims that most applications can be handled by the same broad common languages.

5.4.5 Declaration of Variables

Finally, a few words about declaration of variables. Fortran has implicit declarations, Algol has explicit ones, and APL has dynamic variable creation. Which method is to be preferred?

The difference between Algol and Fortran is syntactic; the variables are there in Fortran as if they were declared. But the APL scheme is different; the variables may or may not appear according to the dynamic behaviour of the program; they may in fact change type in the course of an execution. And the external variables of a procedure may be completely different from call to call. This costs time because means a completely different memory organisation.

So here we found a true pay-off situation: ease of use vs. speed. The dynamic variable creation is a necessary feature in an interpretive language, but I have never felt the need for it in an ordinary programming language, and so am not prepared to advocate it.

It remains to choose between explicit and implicit declarations. The proponents for no declarations argue that declarations are unnecessary, usually they tell no more than can be inferred from the following executable statements. The opponents argue that the declarations force a certain orderliness on the programmer, and that a misspelt identifier will be discovered by the lack of a corresponding declaration. The proponents will come back and argue that for every misspelt identifier you find, you will be dumped off the machine ten times for forgetting declarations. Yes, the opponents retort, but remember how much harder it is to find that misspelt identifier than to complete the declarations.

About the best thing to do would probably be to use the Fortran method, enhanced with a warning if a variable is assigned to and never used, or used but never assigned to. It could be enhanced further by allowing the user to skip the declaration if the variable was initialised by a DATA statement or by an assignment or READ from which its properties could be inferred. That would leave us with the need to declare only those variables that are assigned to by a subroutine call.

5.5 EXPERIMENTAL FEATURES

5.5.1 Exception Handling

The other daily problem in application programming, apart from static arrays, is the handling of exceptions. For many years this was considered outside the scope of standards committees. Now the topic is at least being discussed. The proposals advanced are usually variations of the scheme first used in PL/I. It allows the user to define actions to be taken on different exceptions. The exceptions may be overflow, subscripts out of bounds, I/O errors and the like. The actions usually range over jumps, procedure calls, flag settings, and ignoring the exception. Exceptions that are not explicitly taken care of will abort the execution.

While this is quite an improvement over ignoring the subjects altogether, I am not completely happy about the way things are moving. These schemes do get rather complicated. For one thing, scoping tends to be a problem. The handler will typically only be meaningful in the program unit where it was declared. If that program unit calls another program unit, the handler has to be replicated in the called unit. There seems to be no way of communicating between the handler and the offending statement, e.g. by means of parameters. The handler will therefore tend to be stereotyped. My experience is that each place in the program where an exception can occur needs its own handler. At the very least, the handler must be able to influence the result of the offending statement.

Under a different and simpler scheme proposed below, some important additional facilities could be gained. I am sorry I cannot give a reference to the paper where I read about this sometime in 1959. It was in one of the mainstream computer journals, but I have not been able to locate it.

The idea in brief is this: introduce a function DEFINED(x). This function will have the value .TRUE. or .FALSE. according as x is defined or undefined. Hence the system will have to keep track of which variables are, in fact, defined or undefined.

Pro:

— It will give flexible exception handling and safe programs.
— It is easy to set aside one value to mean 'undefined' for NUMERIC variables. Their representations typically contain an extra value, usually negative zero,

that could be used for this purpose. CHARACTER and BIT variables are even easier since they typically have a length that can be set to -1 or some other, normally impossible value if the variable is undefined.
- It gives an easy and natural way to continue computation.
- No trouble with scopes of event handling procedures.
- It is easy to define; the standard defines a lot of things as being undefined.

Con:
It could be rather time consuming with present hardware, because it would require the elementary arithmetic operations ($+,-,*,/,**$) to give the result 'undefined' if either operand were undefined. It would also require, for example, a permanent check on subscript bounds. The scheme would require new hardware to run fast. (So would the PL/I type handling.)

I have no doubt that the gains in safety and ease of programming would outweigh this, but it is the sort of standard to be phased in over a long period of time.

Using a non-existent subscripted variable in an arithmetic expression should return the result 'undefined' for the variable and hence for the whole expression. In like manner, an overflow should give the value 'undefined' to the expression it appears in. Reading from a file with errors in it or reading beyond end-of-file should set the variables read to 'undefined'.

Under this scheme you have several options for handling errors. You may have the run aborted on error, or you may test results with the DEFINED function and handle each error on its own merits, much as you would do with an overflow test today. But the system would stand guard over you even if you did not handle errors explicitly. Any errors that you ignored, intentionally or by mistake, would propagate down the chain of computation and show up as 'undefined's in the final result. You might not be amused by a result consisting mainly of 'undefined's, but at least you would know the proper results from the spurious ones – a considerable improvement over today's situation.

The most common reason for not handling every error explicitly would be plain convenience. There are often many possible sources of error, each of them highly unlikely, and it would be nice to know that the system would catch them all, without having to clutter up the program with lots of checks. Aborting on the first error is not always the answer, especially if you are checking a lot of input data and want to go on and find the errors on the first run. Or you may wish to run the program to the end, just to see that the result tables look right and have their headings in the right places, even if all the result values are not there yet.

Usually we shall be able to run through a whole program right to the end unless we hit upon an IF statement whose condition is undefined, so we do not know whether to go on after THEN or ELSE, or a DO loop with an undefined number of iterations.

There is no easy way to handle storage outside array bounds. Assuming that we have dynamic arrays, a natural action would be to extend the array, if the storing was done to the element immediately following the last existing element of the array. If the storage was way out of bounds, an error printout would be more appropriate, with no storing taking place.

Once the idea of 'undefined' is established, we can also use it in many algorithms and packages to find out whether a variable is initialised or not. Having the variables undefined initially is, I believe, preferable to having variables initialised with zero.

An interesting side effect of the scheme is that it would give us a standard way of handling the 'missing data' situation so common in statistics.

Having a scheme like the one just described would make many software packages simpler and safer. Packages usually go wrong when the user forgets to initialise. They do also go wrong now and then when arrays within them are overloaded. These errors are typically difficult to find because they tend to make the program 'run wild' without proper error indications. Moreover, you are often at a loss where to look for the error since the package is, or should be, a black box to the user. So, although these errors may not be too frequent, when they do occur they take a lot of time and give packages generally a bad name.

Would a scheme like this cost a lot of machine time? Oh yes, it probably would. Would that time be off-set by cutting programmer time? Yes, in many cases it would, because in many applications machine time is just a fraction of programming costs. At least it would be very nice to have the option. But in the final analysis we have no choice. Programming cost is small compared to the cost of not getting the job done correctly, on time. More and more of our technical work is based on computers. They just have to do the job right.

5.5.2 Controlled Precision Revisited

We have been into this question twice, once in the Fortran portability discussion, once in the Fortran 8X section. Let us recapitulate.

The need for controlled precision decreased a lot with Fortran 77, because generic functions and more general format codes made manual conversion of programs from one precision level to another very much easier.

We need a set of procedures for environmental enquiries, and we are getting them in Fortran 8X.

Further, we need a facility for declared precision, and we are getting that too.

I think the environmental enquiries adopted are good and sufficient for their purpose. I would specifically support both controlled precision and environmental enquiries, because they address different problems. Controlled precision is used when you know what the problem needs, environmental enquiries when you try to get the best out of what machinery and precision you have available.

I also think the simple REAL(PRECISION_10=n) scheme adopted has merit, and pending further insight, it is about as good as we can do. The separate specification of a power of 10 character by REAL_CHAR seems unnecessary, it could be part of the type specification, but that is a minor matter.

Now to the remaining problem areas.

Controlled precision is not so much use if you can't check that you chose the right precision requirement. Let us say your machine has three levels with 6, 12 and 18 decimal digits of precision. Let us further suppose that you believe (wrongly) that 8 digits is enough for your problem and declare your variables REAL(DIGITS=8) X,Y,Z; ... You will get 12 digits on your home computer and the program works fine; not until the program is moved to another machine three years later and actually executed with 8 digits, does it turn out that there are numerical difficulties, and the precision has to be increased.

Therefore, you must be able to check the precision, which you might request with an attribute EXACT. This must insert some programmed floating point package into the program and simulate 8 digits of precision, not only in arithmetic operations, but also in function calls, I/O, etc.

Once you have accepted this mechanism, which means a lot of additions to compiler and library, and a considerable slow-down of execution, you might well wonder 'could not this scheme be used to monitor the arithmetic in a more general and useful way?' Perhaps what we really need is another arithmetic package that keeps track of the actual precision of intermediate and final results and flags critical loss of precision during execution (like subtraction of nearly equal quantities). This is useful for any numerical user, who may in fact not be interested in portability at all, only in getting reliable results. Experiments indicate that the loss of speed need not be prohibitive (factor 3–4 on the operations proper.)

Two final notes on this subject.

The first one concerns ranges for INTEGERs. I am rather surprised this has not become a subject for general discussion. After all, they overflow much more often than REALs, if you use them in computations.

A second note: European experts on numerical computation are now proposing an auxiliary type *dot precision*. This is precision so high that a scalar inner product can be computed with 'complete accuracy'. It can be shown that this can be done with a finite number of bits. This innerproduct function 'dotadd' is fundamental to high precision computation. See [3] for a presentation, with references, of these very interesting ideas.

5.5.3 Miscellaneous Ideas

Finally, I will describe some ideas I have been working with recently but have not really thought through yet. I might as well have called this paragraph 'Half-baked Ideas', but that looks too whimsical for a heading. If you believe in strictness, please go on to the next section.

'Files and arrays are the same thing'

It is actually quite natural to regard files and arrays as the same thing. The difference is mainly historical. We used to think of the file as a set of structured records, available one at a time. We thought of the array as a vector or a rectangular matrix with fixed dimension, all available at the same time. But let us reconsider. Now that we have structured data and variable dimension arrays, we could use the record number of the file as a subscript and (conceptually) convert it into an array of structures. Every field in the file would then become a one-dimensional array. If each record contains a one-dimensional array, the union of these arrays, taken over the whole file would be a two-dimensional array and so on. A lot of operations intended for arrays would become available for files, and vice versa.

There is really no discussion. Let us regard files and arrays as the same thing and start thinking of a common notation for them.

'How do we write an understandable Merge?'

One of the most commonplace and at the same time difficult activities in data processing is to merge or update files. You have to read two files intermittently, keep track of changes in the key or keys they are sorted on and get the effect of end-of-file on either infile right. However carefully you write the merge program it is bound to be difficult to understand, and hence difficult to maintain.

A possible aid to thought might be concepts and ideas from APL. In APL it is easy to describe such things as 'the set of different values of the sort key' or 'all transactions having a certain value of the sort key'. I would love to have the update as two nested loops, the outer one with the sort key running through all values it can take in either file, and an inner loop for transactions with the same key.

There is a nice merge feature in the statistical package SAS [4]. In SAS you can write:

IF LAST.DEPT;

followed by a computation you want to have done only when the current record is the last record for a value of DEPT, i.e. the last record for the department. Is not that very understandable compared to the spaghetti bowl that is the usual merge program?

'Can we get a better file handling generally?'

There are already today many software packages that aid the user in handling files. Systems that come to mind include the statistical package SPSS [5], the information retrieval system INFOL [6], the file handling system AWK [7], and the SAS package just mentioned. These systems have in common that the reading of records, the sensing of end-of-file and a lot of other file handling takes place behind the scenes. The user is only aware of one record at a time and writes the processing (computing, selection, etc.) that is to be done on it. The existence of a subscript – the record number – is implicit.

Can we get something of this simplicity into a language like Fortran, so we can utilise it without using a package?

142

My last wording may sound as if I did not like packages. I must of course object to such an interpretation. But let me say that all battle-hardened programmers share a certain scepticism on this subject.

Packages are fine when all of the following conditions hold.

— The package works.
— The manual is understandable and up to date.
— The printouts are informative.
— The package solves the problem.
— There is someone to ask when you get stuck.

We are always happy to use a subroutine from a well known library. But when the customer puts down a tape on your table and says 'I want you to use this program a friend down South sent me, to make it cheap' . . . the odds are 2 to 1 you are in for trouble.

5.6 SUMMARY

From the above, you may have begun to see what kind of programming language I would like to propose. Let me summarise.

The language should be structured into levels. The difference between two levels should be that the higher level has an important feature (say, recursive procedures) lacking in the lower level, but pays for it in clearly reduced efficiency. The levelling should be orthogonal as far as possible.

The language will be described starting from Fortran 77. It should:

— Retain Fortran's tolerance, in the sense defined above, i.e. an easily handled procedure interface.
— Modularity in the sense that each subprogram can be compiled on its own.

The language should have the following features proposed for Fortran 8X:

— The improved DO and the CASE construct.
— Long identifiers.
— Improved data sharing between program units.
— Keyword parameters.

- Complete types. Any type that exists in the language should be fully supported, i.e. be usable as a function value and have an associated type of constant.
- Recursiveness, as an option.
- Dynamic assigning of array space.
- Precision control.
- Data structures.

The following facilities should be available over and above Fortran 8X:
- The properties of a parameter (type, dimension, etc.) to be easily retrievable from within the subprogram. Variable number of parameters.
- Free placing of name in subprogram calls.
- Subprograms modifiable while program is running.
- Merging of types and operators. The basic character type should be CHARACTER (with dynamic length), retaining present types as options.
- Further implicit declaration of variables.
- Exception handling by the ability to sense and use the value 'undefined'.
- A clean interface to the command language.

5.7 IMPLEMENTATION CONSIDERATIONS

We will soon reach the end of this chapter and this book. Before we do, let us once again look at implementation. If you agree to the ideas set forth in this chapter, what could you do about them? We shall assume that you have access to a Fortran 77 compiler and start from there. As usual, the possibilities vary from feature to feature.

(1) Features that can be implemented by procedure packages:
- Dynamic arrays
- Merging of types
- Experiments in controlled precision
- Experiments in exception handling (the packages above can be combined)
- Access to system variables
- Improved parameter transmission between OS and program

(2) Features that you can implement by preprocessor:
  - Long identifiers
  - Free placing of procedure name
  - Checking procedure interaction and the flow of computation
  - Implicit variable declarations
  - Experiments in file processing

(3) Features requiring a language switch:
  - Improved variable sharing
  - Recursive procedures
  - Dynamic compilation
  - Dynamic creation of variables

(4) Features requiring a new compiler:
  - Variable number of parameters

When I talk of switching to another program language, I am thinking of Simula or APL. Ada would be close to ideal, but experience has taught me never to recommend anything before it is available for trial.

With APL we gain a clean, compact language, but remember the deficiencies mentioned earlier: the lack of communication with other languages, the operator precedence problem, the lack of control constructs and so on. And there is the lower efficiency.

Simula is an interesting alternative. While still not the ideal language, it is better in almost all respects than Fortran 77, except again for efficiency. You really ought to try it and have it as an alternative tool in the many cases when efficiency for the particular run is less important than programming speed. Do not be misled by the name Simula — nowadays simulation is only one of its many applications. Do not be discouraged by sometimes difficult manuals. Try out a subset to start with.

I have put this list of implementation possibilities at the end of this book in order to stress an essential point. In the final analysis, we are responsible for our own methods. We do not have to sit back and wait for standards committees and manufacturers to do everything for us. There is a lot you and I can do at our own installations to advance the techniques of daily programming. We have created tools with enormous capabilities, obedient to the letter, yet somehow unruly. It is time now to make them sit up and do what we mean them to do.

145

5.8 REFERENCES

[1] K. G. Wilson; A Program of Computing Support for Scientific Research; working paper at Cornell University, Ithaca, 1982.

[2] P. Naur (ed.); the *Algol Bulletin;* paragraph 11.4; Regnecentralen, Copenhagen, 1960.

[3] ANS X3J3 Fortran Committee; Minutes of 84th Meeting (X3J3/151), pp. 161–195; 1982.

[4] J. T. Helwig; *SAS Introductory Guide;* SAS Institute Inc., Cary, North Carolina, 1978.

[5] N. H. Nie *et al.; SPSS (Statistical Package for the Social Sciences);* McGraw-Hill; Toronto 1975.

[6] *INFOL-2 Reference Manual;* European Organisation for Nuclear Research; Geneva 1976.

[7] A. V. Aho, B. W. Kernighan & P. J. Weinberger; AWK – A Pattern Scanning and Processing Language; in *Software Practice & Experience,* Vol. 9, pp. 267–279; 1979.

Index

The abbreviations CL and PL are used for command language and programming language, respecively.